Student Handbook to Psychology

Learning and Thinking

Volume IV

Student Handbook to Psychology

Learning and Thinking

Volume IV

BERNARD C. BEINS

CHRISTOPHER M. HAKALA

Facts On File
An Infobase Learning Company

Student Handbook to Psychology: Learning and Thinking
Copyright © 2012 Bernard C. Beins and Christopher M. Hakala

Facts On File, Inc.
An Imprint of Infobase Learning
132 West 31st Street
New York NY 10001

Library of Congress Cataloging-in-Publication Data
Student handbook to psychology / [edited by] Bernard C. Beins.
    v. ; cm.
  Includes bibliographical references and index.
  Contents: v. 1. History, perspectives, and applications / Kenneth D. Keith—v. 2. Methods and measurements / Bernard C. Beins—v. 3. Brain and mind / Michael Kerchner—v. 4. Learning and thinking / Christopher M. Hakala and Bernard C. Beins—v. 5. Developmental psychology / Lynn Shelley—v. 6. Personality and abnormal psychology / Janet F. Carlson—v. 7. Social psychology / Jeffrey D. Holmes and Sheila K. Singh.
  ISBN 978-0-8160-8280-3 (set : alk. paper)—ISBN 978-0-8160-8281-0 (v. 1 : alk. paper)—ISBN 978-0-8160-8286-5 (v. 2 : alk. paper)—ISBN 978-0-8160-8285-8 (v. 3 : alk. paper)—ISBN 978-0-8160-8284-1 (v. 4 : alk. paper)—ISBN 978-0-8160-8282-7 (v. 5 : alk. paper)—ISBN 978-0-8160-8287-2 (v. 6 : alk. paper)—ISBN 978-0-8160-8283-4 (v. 7 : alk. paper) 1. Psychology—Textbooks. I. Beins, Bernard.
  BF121.S884 2012
  150—dc23   2011045277

Text design by Erika K. Arroyo
Cover design by Takeshi Takahashi
Composition by EJB Publishing Services
Cover printed by Yurchak Printing, Landisville, Pa.
Book printed and bound by Yurchak Printing, Landisville, Pa.
Date printed: September 2012
Printed in the United States of America

This book is printed on acid-free paper.

CONTENTS

PREFACE

Behavior is endlessly fascinating. People and other animals are complicated creatures that show extraordinary patterns of abilities, intelligence, social interaction, and creativity along with, unfortunately, problematic behaviors. All of these characteristics emerge because of the way the brain interprets incoming information and directs our responses to that information.

This seven-volume **Student Handbook to Psychology** set highlights important and interesting facets of thought and behavior. It provides a solid foundation for learning about psychological processes associated with growth and development, social issues, thinking and problem solving, and abnormal thought and behavior. Most of the major schools and theories related to psychology appear in the books in the series, albeit in abbreviated form. Because psychology is such a highly complex and diverse discipline, these volumes present a broad overview of the subject rather than a complete and definitive treatise. Such a work, in fact, would be difficult (if not impossible) because psychological scientists are still searching for answers to a great number of questions. If you are interested in delving in more depth into specific areas of psychology, we have provided a bibliography of accessible readings to help you fill in the details.

The volumes in this series follow the order that you might see in a standard presentation on a variety of topics, but each book stands alone and the series does not need to be read in any particular order. In fact, you can peruse individual chapters in each volume at will, seeking out and focusing on those topics that interest you most. On the other hand, if you do choose to read through a complete volume, you will find a flow of information that connects related sections of the books, providing a coherent overview of the entire discipline of psychology.

The authors of the seven volumes in this series are experts in their respective fields, so you will find psychological concepts that are up to date and that reflect the most recent advances in scientific knowledge about thought and behavior. In addition, each of the authors is an excellent writer who has presented the information in an interesting and compelling fashion. Although some of the material and many of the ideas are complex, the authors have done an outstanding job of conveying those ideas in ways that are both interesting and effective.

In *History, Perspectives, and Applications*, Professor Kenneth Keith of the University of San Diego has woven historical details into a tapestry that shows how psychological questions originated within a philosophical framework, incorporated biological concepts, and ultimately evolved into a single scientific discipline that remains interconnected with many other academic and scientific disciplines. Dr. Keith has identified the major figures associated with the development of the field of psychology as well as the social forces that helped shape their ideas.

In *Methods and Measurements*, I illustrate how psychologists create new knowledge through research. The volume presents the major approaches to research and explains how psychologists develop approaches to research that help us answer questions about complex aspects of behavior. Without these well-structured and proven research methods, we would not have much of the information we now have about behavior. Furthermore, these methods, approaches, and practices provide confidence that the knowledge we do have is good knowledge, grounded in solid research.

Many people are under the impression that each thought or behavior is a single thing. In *Brain and Mind*, Professor Michael Kerchner of Washington College dispels this impression by showing how the myriad structures and functions of our brain work in unison to create those seemingly simple and one-dimensional behaviors. As the author explains, each behavior is really the result of many different parts of the brain engaging in effective communication with one another. Professor Kerchner also explains what occurs when this integration breaks down.

Learning and Thinking, co-authored by Professor Christopher Hakala of Western New England College and me (at Ithaca College), explores the fascinating field of cognitive psychology, a discipline focused on the processes by which people learn, solve problems, and display intelligence. Cognitive psychology is a fascinating field that explores how we absorb information, integrate it, and then act on it.

In *Developmental Psychology*, Professor Lynn Shelley of Westfield State University addresses the very broad area of psychology that examines how people develop and change from the moment of conception through old age. Dr. Shelley's detailed and compelling explanation includes a focus on how maturation and environment play a part in shaping how each individual grows, evolves, and changes.

In *Personality and Abnormal Psychology*, Professor Janet Carlson of the Buros Center for Testing at the University of Nebraska (Lincoln) addresses various dimensions of personality, highlighting processes that influence normal and abnormal facets of personality. Dr. Carlson also explains how psychologists study the fundamental nature of personality and how it unfolds.

The final volume in this series is *Social Psychology*. Co-authored by Professor Jeffrey Holmes of Ithaca College and Sheila Singh of Cornell University, this volume examines how our thoughts and behaviors emerge in connection with our interactions with other people. As the authors of this volume explain, changes in a person's social environment can lead to notable changes in the way that person thinks and behaves.

As editor of this series, I have had the opportunity to work with all of the authors who have contributed their expertise and insights to this project. During this collaborative process, I found that we have much in common. All of us have spent our careers pondering why people think and act the way they do. For every answer we come up with, we also develop new questions that are just as interesting and important. And we all agree that you cannot find a more interesting subject to study than psychology.

As you learn about psychology, we hope that the information in these seven volumes inspires the same fascination in you. We also hope that our explanations, illustrations, and narrative studies motivate you to continue studying why we humans are the way we are.

—Bernard C. Beins, Ph.D., Professor of Psychology,
Ithaca College, Series Editor

CHAPTER 1

MEMORY

In the opening chapter of this book, we describe memory, discussing in some detail what psychologists know about the process of memory as well as the research that led to this knowledge. What is amazing, however, is that the information presented here barely scratches the surface of what we know about human memory. This chapter, therefore, is a springboard for further study and discovery rather than a definitive and all-encompassing discussion on this fascinating subject.

In the first component of learning, the act of putting information into memory is called **encoding**, and the act of getting it back out again is called **retrieval**. The simple model of memory looks something like this:

Encoding → Storage → Retrieval

The simplicity of this model is deceptive. In truth, each component in the basic model is a complex process that raises many important questions. For example, what type of encoding leads to better storage? What kind of storage is appropriate for better retrieval? How does retrieval work sometimes and fail at other times? Consider your own memory patterns, for example. Your memory for some things is very good; for other things, it fails miserably. So what are the key differences that give rise to such variability in memory skills? Psychologists have studied this issue extensively.

Memories of Childhood

Let's start with a personal story. When I was a child, I camped with my family at a campground in Massachusetts. I had many fond memories of that campground, including memories of where it was and how long it seemed to take us to get there. In my memory, the ride took hours, and as we reached our destination, the campground was always on the right hand side of the road. As an adult, about 25 years later, I decided to take a ride out to that campground from my parents' house to see the site of my very fond memories (and to decide if I wanted to take my children there as well!). As I was driving, I realized that my memory of the length of the ride was highly inaccurate. The ride itself took only about 45 minutes from my parents' house, not the hours I remembered. And, more to my shock and disbelief, the campground was on the left—that is, on the opposite side of the street from what I remembered! I was amazed. I tried to come up with an explanation for why this was so—even reasoning that the campground may have been relocated across the street. But the fact is, my memory was flawed, as are all our memories.

One reason for this is that humans use a biological entity to remember things about the world (i.e., our brains), and that entity is not a videorecorder, but a physical organ that sometimes does not operate as accurately or as efficiently as we might like it to. In this chapter, as we explore the process of memory, let's keep in mind the fact that we don't always have the ability to directly encode our experiences the way we want to, and even if we do, we don't always have the ability to re-create those experiences as accurately as we hope to.

ENCODING

In early models of memory, encoding was a topic that wasn't discussed very much. The thought was that encoding simply happened and that the important aspect of memory was retrieval. These models of memory were very much centered on the idea of how memory was structured. They focused extensively on organization of long-term memory and how we went about retrieving the information from that memory. However, in 1958, Donald Broadbent proposed a model of information processing that encompassed all aspects of memory in a way that gave rise to extensive revisions in the way psychologists perceived memory. In explaining his model, Broadbent spent a great deal of time talking about how memory was actually the end result of a great deal of work and that there were many steps that led to forming a long-term memory. Broadbent's ideas paved the way for much of the work that occurred in cognitive psychology in the 1960s and especially in the 1970s.

Donald Broadbent's Memory Model

Donald Broadbent described memory as a process of small steps that he hoped would eventually map onto biological processes. His model included several components and looked like this:

$$\text{Sensory register} \rightarrow \text{Filter} \rightarrow \text{Pattern Recognition} \rightarrow \text{attention} \rightarrow \text{STM} \rightarrow \text{LTM}$$

Each stage of his model had different roles and processes, and the ultimate "goal" was a long term memory trace. At the beginning stage, the sensory register, we take in sensory information and store it for a very brief amount of time. The sensory register is a very important part of the process. At any given time, we are being bombarded by literally hundreds of sensory inputs (visual, tactile, auditory, etc.). The information is somewhat overwhelming, so we need a process for storing this sensory input for a very brief period of time. The sensory register allows us to hold sensory information for about 250 milliseconds after the stimulus has disappeared. In that time, we are able to move through a large amount of sensory information and then process additional information as it comes in.

If the information is overwhelming, or if the information is consistent and unchanging, we will filter it out, and it will not be passed on for further processing. There are a great number of stimuli that we DO filter out this way on a regular basis. For example, when you get your ears pierced, you notice the earrings for the first few days. After a while, you stop noticing them. The stimuli are still there. But because they are the same stimuli repeatedly, you stop noticing that they are impinging on the system. As a result, you now have more ability to focus on novel stimuli. The filter serves this purpose very well and makes it easier for us to deal with stimuli that might actually be important to our cognitive system versus stimuli that continually send the same message again and again.

Once stimuli make the way to the pattern recognition stage, we are able to start the process of determining which stimuli we have experienced previously and which are novel stimuli. This process of pattern recognition is interesting, particularly if you consider that we don't really "know" consciously what the stimuli are, but we do have a pretty good sense of whether or not we have experienced them before. This "recognition" helps us decide what we do with such information at the next stage.

The next stage of information processing is attention, which is probably one of the most important and most well understood mechanisms in the system. Attention refers to focusing mental effort on a particular stimulus. Moreover, there are several types of attention. For purposes of this book, we are going to discuss only two of these: focused attention and divided attention.

Focused Attention

Focused attention means that we can devote psychological energy on one particular stimulus and devote those resources to encoding that single stimulus effectively. When we focus our attention, what we are really doing is what we colloquially call "paying attention." Most students are under the impression that humans can pay attention for about 20 minutes before they start to drift. The fact is that research on attention has shown fairly conclusively that students can focus attention for only about 20 seconds before they begin lose focus. Thus, their attention will shift elsewhere and then return to the original stimulus (most of the time). And this happens repeatedly.

Students (and actually all adults) consistently shift attention from one thing to another to another to another. In most cases, however, we cannot really do this effectively nor can we effectively perform multiple tasks. The problem is, of course, that if you are not paying attention to something, you do not remember that thing. Attention is critical for memory. When you pay attention to something, you are actually working on encoding it efficiently into memory so that

Attention in the Classroom

Students are supposed to sit in class and "pay attention" to what is going on, but teachers often do not make this process easy. For one thing, they seldom consider that sitting for a long period of time is difficult for most people. In a classroom, students generally pay attention to the information presented at the beginning of a lecture and at the end of a lecture, but cannot always focus on the information that is presented in the middle of the lecture. Thus, at the point where most teachers would be reaching the critical part of a lecture, the students are not able to focus their attention on the material. If you consider class to be the ideal place for students to learn, this presents a problem.

So what can we do about this? Increasingly, there is research in the scholarship of teaching and learning that suggests that the best way to increase learning is to think of the class as an active, vibrant community. Teachers should provide students with activities, questions, etc., to help students continuously focus their attention on the material at hand. At the same time, students need to learn that the best way to focus on classroom material is to take breaks, to learn to re-orient back to the topic at hand, and to be as active as possible in class.

Although we cannot make all classes stimulating and exciting, the goal of this research is to point out that students are at a definite disadvantage if they are not engaged. A secondary goal is to suggest what teachers and students can do to encourage and maintain engagement.

you can, under the correct circumstances, recall that information again. This cannot happen if your attention is shifting back and forth between two or more sets of material to be learned, because you cannot focus on one thing when you are focusing on another. In addition, it takes time to orient yourself to an alternate task, so you are losing even more information.

The importance of attention and memory is something that magicians are well aware of. As everybody knows, magicians cannot actually make physical objects cease to exist. What they can do, however, is acquire physical skills that make their audiences believe that they can indeed make things disappear and verbal skills that support and enhance that impression. Neuroscientists Stephen Macknic and Susana Martinez-Conde have studied the neuroscience of magic and have pointed out that magicians are truly adept at creating a mindset that leads the audience to focus on one aspect of their behavior while drawing attention away from a crucial behavior. They further note that good magicians are equally adept at using tricks of memory to convince people that one thing happened when, in fact, something slightly different actually happened. The

Research has shown that students have difficulty paying attention during the middle of a long class period. Periodic changes of activity and increases in student engagement can help. (Shutterstock)

discrepancy between what people believe happened and what actually happened is small, but it leads people to put an interpretation on what occurred that is consistent with the magician's intent.

Such reworking of memory can be enjoyable in the context of magic tricks. And most of the time, when it happens to us in everyday life, the implications are minor. But as we will see later in this chapter, there are situations where alterations in memory can have serious consequences.

Divided Attention

Besides understanding the issue of focused attention, it is also important to consider that students often have to divide their attention because they are expected to (or want to) engage in a variety of tasks and activities. Students report that they even do homework under these conditions, trying to complete school projects as they check email, hold phone conversations, watch television, and so forth. Essentially, they are trying to do two or more tasks at one time, with each task requiring some amount of attentional resources, and this pretty much defines the concept of divided attention. Even beyond the classroom, we all have a certain capacity to attend to stimulation around us. If the tasks in which we are engaged are simple enough or highly overlearned, we can complete more than one task because a behavior that we have learned so well that it is automatic does not always place high demands on our attentional capacity. If, however, the tasks are complex or new, it is virtually impossible to devote appropriate levels of attention to all of them at the same time.

Thus, you might be able to combine riding a bike and talking because the motor activity of riding the bike does not require conscious attention. So if you want to ride a bike and talk to your friend, there should not be much of a problem as long as the trail you are biking on is not very demanding. However, if you are riding your bike on a very demanding trail with obstacles you need to watch for and maneuver around, it is far more difficult to do both tasks well because you are now adding another task, one which is not automatic and requires that you devote a considerable amount of your attentional capacity to it. You will not be able to keep talking, maintain your speed on the bike, and successfully navigate the tricky path because to do all three things, you would need to switch your attention rapidly among tasks. In this situation, you have to make a choice regarding where to direct your attention: biking or talking. So you may need to stop talking to your friend or slow down or even stop riding temporarily so that you aren't risking a fall.

This issue of divided attention is a very important one in contemporary life as people try to **multitask**. If we revisit and extend the discussion on students and their various activities, this concept is easy to understand. Interestingly, researchers have shown that students who use instant messaging while studying and doing homework recognize that the instant messaging hampers their ability to complete their work successfully. Fortunately, other research indicates that students may not engage in multitasking to the extent that many people think they do. That is, students who multitask infrequently appear to outnumber those who multitask often.

A related important issue to consider is that you pay attention to the information that is in your short-term memory. Moreover, for something to be part of long-term memory, it must be transferred there (from short-term memory). Without paying attention to something first, you will not have the ability to remember it later on and won't have anything to transfer. Attention, therefore, is the key to long-term memory.

STORAGE
Short–term Memory
In many ways, the ideas that people have about short-term memory are based on the idea that we often forget things. That is, people conceive of short-term memory as something that does not last very long. However, the way psychologists describe short-term memory is very different.

To a psychologist, **short-term memory** is the current contents of memory. That is, whatever you are paying attention to right now is what is in short-term memory. Everything else that you remember, whether it be from recent times or from long ago, is part of long-term memory. Thus, what you had for breakfast is not part of short-term memory even if you just ate breakfast. Rather, it is part of long-term memory. What is in short-term memory is the contents of what you are reading and anything else you might be thinking about at the moment.

Psychologist George Miller pointed out half a century ago that the capacity of short-term memory is very limited. In fact, he argued that the average person could only store about 7 ± 2 bits of information (that is, between 5 and 9 items) at any given time in short-term memory before it became overwhelmed. This result is one of the most consistent in psychological literature. Over time, psychologists have found that this general limitation on the human short-term memory system applies across cultures and across ages. No matter how old you are and no matter what you are trying to remember, once capacity is reached, people tend to have some kind of breakdown in performance.

Short-term memory has been called a variety of other names, including, short-term store, temporary memory, active memory, and working memory. In each of these additional terms, the idea is that short-term memory is really a mental workbench where processing of information happens. Psychologists now recognize that significant mental processing takes place in short-term memory. Alan Baddeley has identified four components of working memory.

(continues on page 10)

A Car Is No Place to Multitask

Many states have passed laws restricting the use of cell phones during driving. In some states, the ban is limited to hand-held phones; hands-free cell phones are still legal in those states. More recently, several states have passed laws that ban texting while driving. There are several overarching reasons for such legislation.

The first is that talking on a cell phone poses difficulties, even for competent drivers. There have been a multitude of studies investigating this question, and the results all point in the same direction: People are less aware of their surroundings when talking on the phone, so they are more prone to accidents. The

Cell phone use while driving poses the same danger as driving while drunk, regardless of whether or not the phone is hands-free. *(Shutterstock)*

risk of driving while on the phone is more or less equivalent to the risk of driving while under the influence of alcohol.

Some argue that using a hand-held cell phone poses more danger than using a hands-free cell phone. Researchers have found, however, that both types of phones are detrimental to driving. On-board systems built into cars may reduce the danger, but even those systems are associated with increases in problems in driving. The problem is not whether a person's hands are free but where a person's attention is going. Thus, the key element concerning this issue revolves around attentional resources.

Figure 1.1 gives an example of how performance changes with cell phone use. With easy driving conditions, people can apply their brakes appropriately, even when using a cell phone. On the other hand, when traffic is heavier, it

(continues)

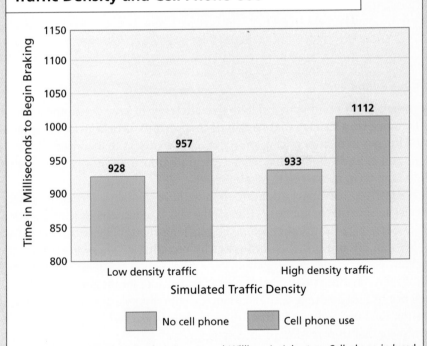

Fig. 1.1 Time to Begin Braking as a Function of Traffic Density and Cell Phone Use

No cell phone / Cell phone use

Low density traffic: 928 / 957
High density traffic: 933 / 1112

Time in Milliseconds to Begin Braking

Simulated Traffic Density

Source: Strayer, David L., Frank A Drews, and William A. Johnston. Cell phone-induced failures of visual attention during simulated driving. *Journal of Experimental Psychology: Applied* 9, no. 1 (March 2003): 23–32. Copyright 2003 American Psychological Association. Adapted with permission.

© Infobase Learning

(continued)

takes longer to respond. The research shows that accidents are more likely when drivers are using cell phones in heavy traffic. This finding should not surprise us: the more traffic there is, the more we attention we have to pay to it, requiring more attentional capacity than we have. So performance deteriorates.

Texting is also highly dangerous. It takes a driver's eyes and attention off the road. Ironically, in states with laws against texting while driving, the accident rate has actually increased. Although the research on this is complicated and still in progress, one possible cause for this anomaly may be that drivers who have continued texting after such laws were passed now place their cell phones in their laps to hide their now-illegal texting, thus increasing the span of time during which they are not looking at the road.

Having a phone conversation or texting is mentally demanding, and people engaged in either of these activities cannot simultaneously attend to good driving practices. The result is that drivers often fail to see important objects (signs, other cars, pedestrians, etc.), and their reaction time to unexpected events is slower than usual. This is a clear recipe for disaster. In fact, research data on this issue suggest that from 2001 to 2007, the number of traffic fatalities resulting from texting was over 16,000.

(continued from page 7)

These include (a) a phonological loop that allows us to keep the sounds in working memory, (b) a visuospatial sketchpad that permits us to keep and manipulate visual images in memory, (c) a central executive system that controls attention, and (d) an episodic buffer that lets us integrate information so we can transfer it into long-term memory.

If a task requires more attention than we have available, we cannot perform that task in short-term memory. Thus, if the task is to remember a long sequence of numbers, once the number sequence gets long enough, performance falters.

We can circumvent this limitation by recoding or *chunking* information together. For example, when people remember their social security numbers, they do not remember them as one long sequence of 9 numbers but rather as a sequence of 3 digits, then 2 digits, then 4 digits. By recoding or chunking the information into larger units that are more densely packed, we are better able to coordinate that information in short-term memory.

In many ways, that is how we overcome similar limitations with language. As we hear words, we tend to group them into grammatical structures, such as phrases or clauses, and chunk those ideas together. If we were not able to do this, understanding sentences longer than a few words would be very difficult, if not impossible.

Long-term Memory

For much of the cognitive activity you conduct in your life, long-term memory is required. Long-term memory contains much more than just your memory for what happened to you in the past. In fact, psychologists have identified several aspects of memory processes that are associated with different elements of long-term memory. For example, one distinction psychologists have drawn is between **episodic** and **semantic memory**. Episodic memory is autobiographical memory—specifically, your memory for events that happened to you in your life. The important distinction for this type of memory is that episodic memories tend to be tied to particular points in your personal history.

Semantic memory, on the other hand, is your general store of other knowledge that might help you in your day-to-day activities. For example, memory for what words mean is contained in semantic memory. It is unlikely that people will remember actually learning the meaning of any particular word, but they will remember the meaning. And, along with the meaning comes the pronunciation, the part of speech, and so forth. The information that is in semantic memory is information that is sometimes called *general world knowledge*. It is information that most people know but that is not tied to any particular time or place. The information in semantic memory is crucial for the development of additional knowledge because the existing information helps new learning occur.

Another distinction sometimes drawn from within the broad category of long-term memory is that of **declarative** versus **procedural knowledge.** Declarative knowledge is knowing something (i.e., the facts of something), whereas procedural knowledge is knowing how to do something. We are sometimes able to separate these two types of knowledge and be able to do something without understanding how we do it (e.g., speaking).

Yet another distinction could also be used to explain the phenomenon described above. Over the past 20 years, psychologists have drawn a distinction between implicit and explicit memory. Implicit memory is a type of memory process in which a person's previous experiences affect a current task without the person's awareness of those previous experiences. A common example of implicit memory involves a person's being primed without awareness to think of some concept, then in a later task, the person performs differently because of the prior exposure.

All of these distinctions are drawn for purposes of enabling pertinent questions about memory. The distinctions are not meant to be exclusive and they are not meant to be taken as real "things." Rather, they are guidelines for how we can effectively ask questions about how memory works. Asking those questions, may help us develop theories that will allow us to better predict how memory is likely to work under different conditions.

Occasionally, psychologists encounter people with exceptional abilities to encode information almost effortlessly. One such person, Laurence Kim Peek, was able to memorize an entire page of names and telephone numbers from a telephone directory in a just few seconds. He was the real-life inspiration for the **savant** characterized in the movie *Rain Man*. Interestingly, he was born without a corpus callosum, a bundle of neurons that connect the right and left hemispheres of the brain, which can be associated with exceptional abilities. Scientists still do not know how or why such skills develop, although they are often accompanied by social deficits.

Encoding Specificity

Earlier in this chapter, we discussed the process of encoding. As defined, encoding is the process of taking in information from the environment and transferring it to long-term memory for later use. This process is tremendously complex and involves a variety of complicated steps. However, the encoding process is also fascinating and unbelievably efficient, helping us remember quite a lot and in a number of very important ways.

What steps are required to transfer information from short-term to long-term memory? The research on this topic has suggested that the more work that is done on processing information, the better chance the information has of being remembered for the long term. Thus, if you devote a great deal of attention to something, it increases the probability that you will eventually be able to remember that information again at a later date. However, it is more complicated than that. Sometimes, even in situations in which attention is devoted to something, a lack of integration can mean that the information involved will be remembered only under certain conditions or in certain situations.

Psychologists recognize that when we engage in learning, we remember more than those things that we are trying to encode. That is, we also encode the environment in which we are learning, our physical state, and so forth. When trying to retrieve learned information from memory at a later time, we can be more successful when all of the cues present when we learned are also present during the retrieval process. This effect is known as **encoding specificity,** which means that the context in which information is learned is critical for the recall of that information. That is, if you reinstate the context in which you originally learn the material, you are more likely going to remember that information.

One clever demonstration of this effect involved scuba divers who learned a list of words in one of three different environmental contexts: on shore, next to water, or while 20 feet underwater. The divers were then to be tested on the words learned. Half of the people in each group learned the words and were tested in the same context (e.g., learned and tested next to water), whereas half learned the words and were tested in different contexts (e.g., learned underwater and tested on shore). As the investigators predicted, recall was better when the divers were asked to recall the words in the context in which they had learned them. The effect of the learning context was dramatic and significant.

A relatively recent addition to models of storage includes the idea of **connectionist networks**. According to the connectionist model, a memory is associated with a pattern of activation of interconnected networks, not single nodes. The strength of a memory is associated with the strength of the connections.

RETRIEVAL AND FORGETTING
Retrieval
It is not unusual to know something but have difficulty recalling it. Quite often, in fact, when people are on the verge of recalling something, they may say that it is "on the tip of their tongue," but they cannot quite get it. This experience reflects one of the fascinating elements of retrieval from long-term memory: When we remember a particular idea, we are really assembling a set of memory fragments that ultimately emerge as a single, unified concept. Most of the time, we are not aware that we are assembling these fragments because we are usually so proficient at the retrieval process. It is only when memory begins to break down that we are aware of some of the individual, hidden aspects of memory.

One effective demonstration of this process involves the **tip-of-the-tongue (TOT) phenomenon**. Psychologists Roger Brown and David McNeill investigated this phenomenon in the laboratory in a very clever way. (They had to be clever because it is hard to generate the TOT state on the spur of the moment. Most of the time, our memories are fairly accessible.)

The researchers presented to a group of participants a set of definitions of words that the participants might know but that are relatively rare in everyday use. Brown and McNeill, for example, would ask participants to identify the word for "a small, flat-bottomed Chinese boat used for fishing and sometimes for housing." (The word is *sampan*.) Participants hearing definitions like this often reported that they knew the word but couldn't retrieve it. But even though they could not say the word, they could often produce information about the word, such as that it had two syllables, began with an *s*, and ended with an *n*.

As you can see, it would be difficult to generate the TOT state reliably because you would need a collection of words that people know but that are hard to access. Moreover, such words will differ from one person to the next. Nonetheless, Brown and McNeill (and many other researchers following their lead) have been successful in documenting the characteristics of the TOT state. Further investigation has led to the conclusion that young people experience the TOT state once or twice a week and older adults about two to four times a week.

Enhancing Retrieval
One way to increase the likelihood that you will be able to retrieve information from memory is to recreate the context in which you learned it. By putting

Encoding Specificity in School

At the beginning of every semester, students enter the classroom and sit down. The teacher then starts calling the roll. Sometime after a few class meetings, the teacher is able to remember the students' names with relative ease. This is a very common pattern in colleges and high schools, and it gives students some comfort to know that a teacher knows them by name.

Now imagine that a student is in a grocery store and sees a teacher who has addressed him or her by name in class several times. The student says hello and is surprised to discover that the teacher cannot remember his or her name. What has happened?

What has happened is that the teacher remembers the student's name only under the appropriate conditions in which the information was learned. It is more than likely that the teacher will always remember the student's name in class because students tend to sit in the same seat and because the context is unchanged. If the context changes, however, the teacher must rely on other cues to help him or her recall the student's name. In a grocery store and in other environments that are not directly related to school, there are often not enough of these cues, and thus the teacher will fail to remember students' names.

To increase the probability of remembering something, it is best to learn things in greater detail with a wider range of context. As Figure 1.2 illustrates, *school* would be the easiest concept (and context) for teachers and for students because it has the most connections and provides the most cues. In general, if a concept is well integrated into a network of ideas, it is more easily recalled than if it is only tangentially connected.

If we assume that concepts farther away from *school* would be harder to remember than a central idea would be, then something only loosely related to

yourself into the same environment during retrieval that you were in during learning, you can improve your recall. This phenomenon is associated with **context-dependent memory**. In fact, researchers have demonstrated that simply by thinking about the context in which they learned something was enough to improve their recall.

A second way to improve recall is by putting yourself in the same bodily state during recall as you were in during learning. So if you are going to take a test during the morning, it makes sense to study during the morning because your body is likely to be in the same state in both instances. This phenomenon is associated with **state-dependent memory**.

You can also enhance your memory by using **mnemonic devices**, processes that are designed to help you encode, then retrieve, information. Mnemonic school (like a person's name) might be harder to recall because it is so far from the main concept of school. Ideas closer to the concept (and context) of school are more easily accessible because they are so close to the concept. Concepts that are less closely related to the central idea pose more of a challenge. If we continually interact with people under a variety of conditions, their names will become more centrally located within the memory scheme and will be more easily recalled under different conditions.

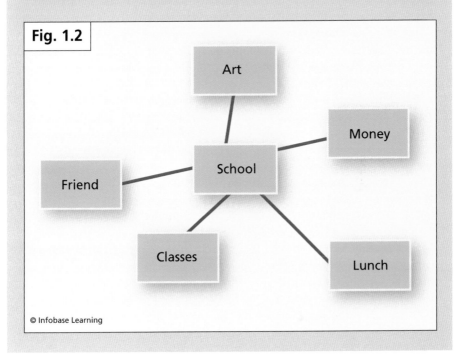

Fig. 1.2

© Infobase Learning

devices help attach meaning to the information you want to remember, and meaningfulness is associated with improved memory.

Two commonly used mnemonic strategies are the **method of loci** and the **pegword method**. To use the method of loci to help you remember a list of items, you imagine walking in a familiar area, like through your house. As you mentally walk through the area, you put one object in a certain location, then a second object to be remembered in a second location, and so on. In retrieval, you retrace your steps and pick up the objects. In general, the more unusual the visual imagery you use, the better your retrieval will be.

In the pegword method, you use a rhyme, like *One is a bun, two is a shoe, three is a tree, four is a door,* and so on. Then you connect a series of items in a list with an image you create. So if the first word in a list is *car* and your rhyming words are one and bun, you might picture a "car sandwich"; if the second word on the list is *cloud*, you might imagine two shoes walking on top of a fluffy cloud, and so on. As with the method of loci, when you want to

The Miracle of a Perfect Memory: Blessing or Curse?

Imagine being able to remember everything you ever came into contact with. If you never forgot anything, what would your world be like? Russian psychologist Alexander Luria studied a man named Solomon Veniaminovich Shereshevsky for many years, referring to him simply as *S*. This man forgot almost nothing, and decades after Luria first met him, S could recount with accuracy material learned many years before.

S had the gift of a very visual memory. When he tried to remember something, it was very often associated with visual images that he created. In fact, on the rare occasions when he omitted something from a list that he was to learn, there was a visual explanation: He would use the method of loci to "place" the item to be remembered in a particular location. S might miss it later when he later mentally retraced his steps during recall, but only if that place was dark. Moreover, he virtually never remembered something inaccurately.

Part of S's visual sense was connected to **synesthesia**, which is a mixing of the senses. When he heard voices, for example, he also saw visual images. When he met another famous Russian psychologist, Lev Vygotsky, he commented, "What a crumbly, yellow voice you have." And when he encountered the number 8, he said that "it has a naïve quality, it's milky blue." These types of visual images were consistent each time he heard that voice or saw that number.

S ultimately became a mnemonist, a person who performs on stage by remembering long lists of words, numbers, or syllables that people in the audience give him. He worried, though, that over time, the lists would crowd one another in memory, so he taught himself how to forget, which is not something most people can do.

The downside of this spectacular memory was that S attended to the characteristics of the words and sounds without processing the meaning of what he was hearing. If somebody spoke or read too fast, the images would crowd and bump into one another and S would have difficulty getting the point. In addition, when he faced homonyms, like the bank of a river and the bank where you get money, he would often become confused.

The visual images that S conjured up were as real to him as the world that we see when we look around. But it was because of this "mixed blessing" that he had difficulty living simultaneously in his visual world and the real world around him.

retrieve the items, you simply access the pegwords and the images associated with them.

As you can see, these mnemonic strategies rely on a preplanned structure onto which you attach items to be remembered. With practice, it is possible to become very proficient at remembering significant amounts of material.

Forgetting

Just as psychological scientists have studied how people encode, store, and retrieve information, they have spent a lot of time trying to figure out why people forget. It is pretty clear that sensory memory is fragile and that the simple passage of time causes input to decay and memory to diminish very rapidly. Similarly, short-term working memory is limited in capacity, so if it is overburdened, memory fails.

In contrast, long-term memory seems to have no particular time limit or capacity. We can remember innumerable things from days, weeks, months, and years ago. Still, forgetting is a reality that we all face on a regular basis.

There are three potential explanations for failure to remember something that we have learned. One possible factor is interference. That is, after being exposed to information, our memories might falter if we come up against new, related information. In fact, this type of interference, called **retroactive interference**, does lead to diminution in memory. Similarly, if we learn something and then subsequently try to learn new information, the information learned earlier will affect memory for the later information, a phenomenon called **proactive interference**.

A second cause of forgetting is **retrieval failure**. As discussed earlier, if the context changes or if one's state changes from learning to recall, memory is impaired even if the information we want to retrieve still exists somewhere in our memory.

A third possible reason for forgetting, one which psychologists have studied but have generally rejected, is decay. That is, the passage of time alone does not seem to affect our memories. Interference and retrieval failure seem to be the most critical factors when we cannot remember something.

Finally, we know that forgetting is not simply the opposite of remembering. That is, you can work to remember something by rehearsing it, elaborating on it, and so forth. But most people cannot forget on cue. If you learn something and somebody asks you to forget it, you will most likely not be able to. Different mental operations are at work in learning and forgetting.

THE FRAGILE NATURE OF MEMORY

Reports of satanic rituals and sexual abuse of children shocked the United States in the 1980s. Adults began recalling that they had been victims of satanic rituals, and the alleged perpetrators were sometimes jailed. This phenomenon of the sudden reappearance of memories from childhood led to the **recovered memory controversy**.

The problem involved supposed traumatic experiences that children underwent, subsequently repressing their memories of those events. It turned out that a relatively small number of psychotherapists and psychiatrists were associated with a large proportion of the clients who were said to have recovered their memories of abuse. And when researchers tried to document such cases of abuse, the evidence generally seemed not to be there. (One important thing to remember here is that sexually abused children do not typically repress such memories. Thus, although it is possible that memories may be repressed, such repression does not seem to figure into the sensational cases of so-called recovered memory.)

But what could cause people to "remember" events that did not happen? Psychologists have addressed this issue in research and have discovered some potential causes for such false memories. One phenomenon to which we can all fall prey is called the **misinformation effect**. If we witness some event, information that we get about that event afterward can affect our memories about what happened. So even when that after-the-fact information is wrong, we incorporate it into our memory schema, which affects the memories we previously constructed. In fact, psychologists have coined the term **reconstructive memory** to explain the idea that we do not store intact memories; instead, we reconstruct memories that include varied elements, some of which are not actually associated with the event that we are trying to remember.

One of the problems with false memories is that they become indistinguishable from real memories. That is, we alter what we remember based on what may happen after an event, based on misinformation about the event, and based on what we actually recalled about the event.

CONCLUSION

As is clear from the information in this chapter, memory is very complex process. It is not merely a digital recording of events as they unfold, but rather a complex series of steps that give rise to the sometimes fleeting thoughts and ideas that we carry around with us. From the very strong memories we have of what words mean, to the fleeting memories we have from when we were children, it is an incredible process that continues to cause psychologists to rethink how they conceptualize the process. In the coming years, the way we understand memory processes will continue to change and evolve as new research results are discovered and described.

At this point, we have a fairly good understanding of many of the phenomena of sensory memory, which involves the initial stages of information processing; encoding, the initial stages of integration of ideas; and retrieval and forgetting. There are still many questions that we need to address, including why our memories are sometimes so robust and sometimes so fragile.

Further Reading

Cytowic, Richard E. *The Man Who Tasted Shapes. A Bizarre Medical Mystery Offers Revolutionary Insights into Emotions, Reasoning, and Consciousness.* New York: Putnam, 1993.

Loftus, Elizabeth F. "Planting Misinformation in the Human Mind: A 30-year Investigation of the Malleability of Memory." *Learning & Memory* 12, no. 4 (Jul 2005): 361–366.

Luria, A.R., and Lynn Solotaroff. *The Mind of a Mnemonist: A Little Book About a Vast Memory.* Cambridge, Mass.: Harvard University Press, 1987.

CHAPTER 2

REASONING AND PROBLEM SOLVING

We encounter situations every day that require us to solve problems and make some kind of decision. Most of these are minor, like whether we should wear a heavy coat because it is cold now or a light coat because it will be warm later. Or what route we should take in completing errands when the usual route is under construction. Most of the time, we don't consider such things problems to be solved because they are so mundane and unimportant.

Nonetheless, each decision we make depends on a set of cognitive processes in which we balance advantages and disadvantages and deal with some measure of uncertainty as we look for the best strategy or most useful conclusion. We might in fact use the same mental processes for trivial decisions as we would for important decisions. In the latter case, however, we might be more aware of the factors that inform our choices.

Psychologists have spent a century studying how we reason and arrive at decisions and what strategies we use in solving problems. As a result, we know a lot about the mental processes that influence our decisions. Sometimes our mental processes lead us to good choices, but sometimes they lead us astray.

The seemingly automatic processes of thinking are really very complex. Reasoning and problem solving are no different. A simple decision results from a combination of different factors, including what we know (or think we know), how a question or problem is framed, our level of expertise, and strategies that we have used in the past.

Judgment and Decision Making

The initial conceptualization of human decision making was that people were entirely rational. The first formal model specified that people know all of their options and the likely outcomes about behavior, that they can make very fine distinctions regarding outcome differences as a result of their choices, and that they are fully rational in the decisions they make. This was initially called the model of the economic man.

This model might provide an excellent description of human decision making if life were simple. Unfortunately, in the real world, people are often ignorant about possible choices and the outcomes that result from them, they can't and don't always make very fine distinctions regarding how their choices will affect outcomes, and even when they know a lot and can figure out likely outcomes, they make irrational decisions. Table 2.1 presents a few real-life examples of decisions people face and shows how and why the real-life processes rarely conform to the economic man model.

TABLE 2.1.
Decision Making in Economic Man Model vs. Decision Making in Real Life

Example: Which college should I attend?	
Element of the economic man model	**How real life violates the economic man model**
Knowledge of all options and outcomes	It is impossible to know all options (i.e., colleges or even all colleges that offer what student wants). It is also impossible to know what all the outcomes would be as a result of choosing College A versus College B because there are too many unknown and unpredictable factors that are likely to affect the outcome.
Sensitive to distinctions among varied outcomes	There is no way to make fine discriminations about which outcome would be best because outcomes are multilayered. Choosing College A would lead to better outcomes on some things but not on others.
Rational with regard to choices	Even when some outcomes are clear, people make their decisions on the basis of emotional factors (i.e., the weather was better when I visited College A, so I will go there; all my friends are going to College B, so I will go there).

A big part of the problem with decision making involves uncertainty. We often do not know as much as we would like to know (or need to know) about many decisions we need to make. Consequently, decision making is often a matter of guesswork based on what is known and hope that what is known is correct and sufficient for making a good decision. Those guesses are only as useful as the information that we know or think we know.

An alternative model to the economic man model is based on **subjective expected utility**. This model suggests that people make decisions based on the combination of the expected payoffs available with each choice and the likelihood that a particular outcome will result from a given choice. Given that we are talking about human behavior, it is not surprising that people generally do not conform to this model either. People tend not to be as systematic as this model stipulates.

A further extension to both of these models involve the idea that people show **bounded rationality,** a concept positing that people act rationally, but only to a degree. Psychologist and economist Herb Simon proposed that people's logic in making decisions is based on limited knowledge, their cognitive ability in assessing relevant factors, and limited time in which to make a decision. Within the boundaries of these limitations, according to Simon, people are as rational as they can be in some cases but emotional or irrational in others.

Because all of the models described here are unrealistic or limited or otherwise flawed, psychologists have identified a variety of different factors associated with making choices. These factors do not yet fall into an overall model that characterizes behavior across the situational board, but they have merit when applied in a variety of circumstances. Arguably the most important aspect of these factors is that they all take into account the fact that people are imperfect deciders.

HEURISTICS AS AIDS TO DECISION MAKING

With all of the possible decisions we make every day, it makes sense that we would rely on shortcuts whenever possible. Otherwise, we would spend the day buried in thought and doing nothing. Psychologists have investigated extensively the nature of the shortcuts that people use in decision making.

One way to arrive at a correct solution to a problem is to use an **algorithm**, a strategy that tests all possible outcomes until the correct one is reached. It leads to guaranteed success because the strategy generates a process that exhausts all possibilities. This strategy will be successful, but it may not be terribly efficient because there might be too many different possibilities to examine.

Consider, for example, the case of trying to remember your password for a particular computer application. You might have quite a few different passwords

Decision Making: Can You Get Rich at the Casino?

Gambling casinos are a big business in the United States and in many other countries. People go to these casinos for a variety of reasons, but the primary reason is to try their luck (or skill) at games of chance and hopefully go home with piles of money. But what expectations do people really have about this outcome.

On occasion, someone will win a large amount of money, whether it be through skill or luck or a combination of the two. But in the long run, most people lose their money. Over time, luck plays no role in the outcome because the outcomes of the games are based on statistical probabilities, not luck.

An American roulette wheel has a payoff structure that guarantees bettors will lose in the long run. Even knowing the odds of winning big money are slim, people continue to make the decision to play. (Conor Ogle. Wikipedia)

for different applications, so you can't remember one for an application that you haven't used for a while. Some systems will lock you out if you attempt to enter more than a few times using the wrong password. The programmers are assuming that somebody may be trying to access your account without your permission. Obviously, entering all the different passwords you have ever used is not a good idea (partly because the system would lock you out and partly because it is likely to be excessively time consuming). It would be better to figure out what

For instance, at a roulette wheel in an American casino, there are 18 numbered red slots and 18 numbered black slots, which means there are 36 numbered slots that could lead to a win. If the roulette ball landed in the slot you chose, you would win $35 for your bet. So if you bet $1 on every single possible winning number (which nobody would really do), you would have bet a total of $36. If the ball landed on any one of those 36 numbers, you would get to keep your initial bet and would also receive the $35 payoff.

This outcome seems like an even bet. But it isn't because there are two additional slots, labeled 0 and 00, that are automatic wins for the casino. (European roulette wheels have only one such slot.) The ball will not land there often (only about 5.3 percent of the time), but when it does, none of the bettors win anything. In the long run, this is the percentage of the money bet that the casino is going to get on any given trial.

So why do people flock to casinos to gamble even if they know their chances of losing are pretty much guaranteed and that good luck doesn't much matter because the house is going to win in the long run? It all comes down to the psychology of decision making. Sometimes they think they can win because they have seen other people win. Sometimes they simply believe that they can beat the odds. And sometimes they fall prey to the so-called **gambler's fallacy**, the belief that they are "due" to win because they have lost a lot already, so their number will come up. (Unfortunately, this is not the way the probabilities work.)

Moreover, the payoffs in gambling are on a variable ratio schedule, which means that the person's behavior is reinforced (i.e., the person wins some money) on occasion. In a given game, the reinforcement (i.e., the win) may occur after a few bets or after many, so that in the long run, the person wins once every 10 times. Different games of chance have different reinforcement schedules.

Once a behavior is established on a variable ratio schedule, it is difficult to extinguish. As a result, gamblers continue to gamble without really being aware of the reason they are doing so. No matter what they base their decisions on and no matter which game of chance they play, the odds favor their leaving the casino with less money in their pockets than when they entered.

strategy you used to create the password and thus narrow down the possibilities. Refining the algorithm also means you have created a shortcut to solve the problem.

When you make use of a shortcut in the decision-making process, you are using a **heuristic**. The shortcut doesn't guarantee that you will arrive at the correct solution to a problem, but it does make the process of arriving at a decision easier.

Suppose you are going to buy a pair of athletic shoes. You could try on every single pair in every style that comes in your foot size. But if you really dislike shopping, you might simply start trying the shoes and stop at the first pair that is acceptable, even if there might be more comfortable shoes that you have not sampled. If your strategy is to pick the first acceptable choice, you are engaging in a heuristic called **satisficing**.

As with any heuristic, it could lead to a good decision (e.g., you have a pair of shoes that you are satisfied with) or a poor decision (e.g., you missed out on a different style that would have fit you better). The important point here is that you used a strategy that led to a decision and you have a pair of shoes.

When you arrive at a conclusion based on incomplete information (e.g., you don't know if there are better shoes that you did not try) you are engaging in **inductive reasoning**. Such reasoning involves using the information that you already have and trying to make a good decision in a new or uncertain situation. Obviously, you are often able to make good guesses: If you want to cross a street and a traffic light is green in your direction, you use inductive reasoning to conclude that cars coming up to a red light are going to stop because that is what has happened in the past. We make decisions like this all day, every day, without recognizing that we are engaging in inductive reasoning.

Reasoning that involves certainty, like mathematical proofs, involve **deductive reasoning**. You can prove that the sum of the squares of the legs of a right triangle equals the square of the hypotenuse. But in conditions of uncertainty, like human behavior, you can only make predictions that might be correct. Scientific research invariably relies on inductive reasoning.

Psychological scientists have studied various heuristics in great detail. Several of these are briefly described above; two other common heuristics are presented below in greater detail. Note that they do not exhaust all of the possibilities associated with making decisions.

Representativeness Heuristic

Imagine that you flipped a normal coin ten times. What outcome would be most likely from among these three:

a) ten heads,
b) ten tails, or
c) this sequence: H H T T T H T H T H?

Most people are likely to guess that the third outcome is the most likely of these three. In reality, all three outcomes are equally likely. (It is true that five heads and five tails is the most likely *combination* of heads and tails, but the particular sequence shown above is no more likely than any other sequence.)

Psychologists have used the **representativeness heuristic** to describe why most people choose the third option of the three presented in the example on flipping coins. The reason is that people associate coin flips with variable outcomes from one flip to another. They believe that a random process of coin flipping looks more like the third alternative than ten heads or ten tails would. Based on this belief, the third alternative seems to be the outcome that looks most representative of the result of ten coin tosses.

Psychologists Amos Tversky and Daniel Kahneman studied this heuristic (and others) and found that, although it could lead to useful decisions, it could also lead to errors. For example, if you learned that a man named Irving was shy but pleasant, wore glasses, and spent his leisure time reading, would you conclude that this person was more likely to be a librarian or a salesman? Tversky and Kahneman posed questions like this to research participants and found that people tended to think that the person was a librarian. This outcome is entirely consistent with the representative heuristic because the personality characteristics described here are representative of what people think a librarian is like. In addition, you might have decided that somebody named Irving is likely to be a librarian rather than a salesman, but what you have not considered is that when parents name a child, they do not know what occupation their offspring will ultimately select, so a person's name really tells you more about the parents than about the person in question.

Irving might indeed be a librarian, but it is much more likely that he is a salesman because there are about 75 times as many salesmen in the United States (where Tversky and Kahneman conducted their research) as there are librarians. What is happening in this example (in addition to the issue of representativeness) is that people are ignoring (or are simply unfamiliar with) **base rates**. That is, they are ignoring the fact that there are many more salespeople than there are librarians. People quite often do not know base rates; even if they do, however, they sometimes ignore them and go for what "feels right"—in this case deciding that Irving is a librarian.

Another way that the representativeness heuristic can lead to less than optimal conclusions involves the **conjunction fallacy**. Suppose that a person alternates between being easygoing, articulate, and funny at one point and manic and almost out of control at another. Is it more likely that this person is an actor, or an actor who is using illegal drugs?

After the example of Irving the salesman above, you might be cautious in making a decision in this second case. But you might be tempted to conclude that the person is an actor who is using drugs. Again, it is possible that your conclusion is right, but it is less likely that the person is an actor who is using

Fig. 2.1 The Conjunction Fallacy

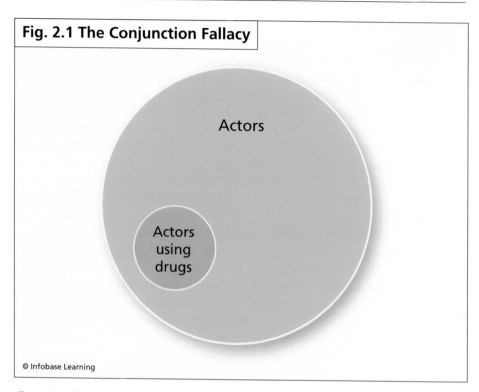

Actors

Actors
using
drugs

© Infobase Learning

Illustration of conjunction fallacy. It would be impossible for there to be more actors using drugs (a subset) than actors (the complete set). Nonetheless people may be more likely to say that a person is an actor using drugs than simply an actor.

drugs than simply an actor. As Figure 2.1 shows, actors using drugs are a subset of all actors, so if this person is using drugs, the person is still an actor. It would be impossible for there to be more people in the subset than in the complete set.

Although these examples may suggest that using the representative heuristic leads to poor conclusions, this heuristic can actually be quite useful in real life, but that generally depends on the information you have to work with. For instance, if you knew that Irving in the example above was dyslexic and had difficulty reading, you would probably guess "salesman" rather than "librarian." On the other hand, if you learned that Irving disliked dealing with financial matters, you might be correct in guessing "librarian." In each case, your answer is more likely to be correct than answers based on the name Irving.

Or if we revisit the street-crossing example above, your heuristic is that drivers pay attention to traffic lights because that is part of your experience. So you decide that it is safe to cross the street when they have a red light and you have a green light and in most cases, you would be correct.

The few examples presented here illustrate that making decisions based on representative heuristics is part of the daily fabric of life but generally not something people do consciously. For most decisions we make every day, it would not make any sense (and it would be terribly inefficient) to stop and consider every aspect of every choice.

The reason that heuristics are dismissed as strategies that lead to erroneous conclusions is that psychologists like to study situations where strategies apply and where they break down. One criticism of psychological research on heuristics is that it focuses on biases and errors in thought whereas the heuristics that we use are reasonably efficient most of the time. It is only when psychologists study artificial problems in laboratories that the deficiencies in the use of heuristics stand out.

Availability Heuristic

In some aspects of our lives, we encode information automatically. This phenomenon was demonstrated by psychologists Lynn Hasher and Rose Zacks, whose research showed that people keep track of how often events occur without overt awareness that they are doing so. This fact suggests that in later processing of information, people should be able to make use of frequency of occurrence in their judgments about events in everyday life.

In fact, when people try to recall information, they are highly affected by frequency information. So if you tried to guess which of two events is more common, in many cases you would be able to do so. However, as with the representativeness heuristic, psychologists have created situations to demonstrate when this automatic counting mechanism breaks down.

One approach is to ask people which is a more common cause of death, tornadoes or asthma? Suicide or homicide? People are quite likely to respond that tornado deaths outnumber asthma deaths even though asthma deaths can be 80 times more common; this pattern holds true even in years with extremely high numbers of tornado deaths. Similarly, people are likely to believe that death by homicide are more prevalent than death by suicide when, in reality, suicides are nearly twice as common.

If we are generally good at encoding the frequency with which events occur, what explains the significant error rate in estimating likelihood of causes of deaths? The answer relates to the **availability heuristic**, which is a general approach we use in deciding about events. We are likely to focus on how easily examples come to mind and base our judgments on ease of recall.

Take the case of tornado deaths. When a tornado takes the lives of a handful of people, it makes the news, perhaps even the national news if the tornado is severe enough and the death toll is high enough. In contrast, we virtually never hear about asthma deaths, unless the information is in a personal context (friend, colleague, neighbor, etc.). In a similar vein, we regularly hear news reports about murders, but news reports almost never mention suicides unless some famous person is involved.

So in some cases, the availability heuristic can lead us astray in judging how frequently something occurs. In spite of this, as psychologist Gerd Gigerenzer has argued, we use "fast-and-frugal" heuristics in everyday life, and these are remarkably useful because they tend to be accurate. In fact, research has supported the claim that these so-called fast-and-frugal heuristics can lead to decisions that are every bit as good as decisions reached via more complicated strategies.

We shouldn't be too surprised that quick and efficient heuristics work. After all, people have been using them ever since there have been decisions to be made, which is to say forever. If you doubt this, consider prehistoric times. If people hadn't developed the ability to use fast-and-frugal heuristics, it is doubtful that they would have lived long enough to reproduce. Viewed in this light, heuristic abilities may have an evolutionary basis that has served humanity well since time immemorial.

Limitations in Decision Making

Traditional models of decision making posited that people were rational and made decisions based on information and logic. We now understand that in many situations, we do not have complete information or may make use of strategies that are not optimal in drawing appropriate conclusions. In addition, it is clear that emotions play a role in decisions that people make.

So even though most of the heuristics we use on an everyday basis are somewhat helpful, there are still some systematic ways that we can end up with erroneous conclusions. Psychologists have identified several common factors that impair our ability to arrive at appropriate decisions.

Emotions and Decision Making

People like to think that their decisions are motivated by logic and rationality, but psychologists have shown that our emotions have an impact on many of the decisions we make. One example of this is the way **incidental emotions**, feelings that are not relevant to a decision, can influence us.

Psychologist Uri Simonsohn has investigated the role of emotions in decision making and has pointed out that emotions have an impact in three particular ways. First, mood affects the way that information is processed. For example, people experiencing positive moods make more use of heuristics whereas people experiencing negative moods tend to be more analytical. Secondly, people can access memories formed when they were in a given mood better if they are in that mood when trying to remember. Finally, people use their moods as salient information that affects a decision (even when the mood is not relevant to the decision).

The real question, however, is whether the effects of mood that researchers have documented in laboratory settings are relevant to real-world behavior. Simonsohn's research has shown that these effects can indeed be quite substantial. For example, he studied the outcome of college admissions committees and found that the committee in the institution he studied paid more attention to academic characteristics of applicants when it was cloudy and more attention to nonacademic characteristics when it was sunny. Similarly, he found that prospective students who visited the university on a cloudy day were more likely to attend that school than if they visited on a sunny day.

We all know that the weather can affect our mood. But research like this shows that emotions and mood can affect cognitive processes that we think are governed by logic. An interesting factor is that we may not even be aware of the role of emotion in our decisions.

Framing

Sometimes our decisions are affected by the way information is presented to us. That is, by the way that the information is framed.

For instance, psychologists have speculated that people have evolved to be sensitive to how often an event occurs but not to the more abstract notion of the probability that an event will occur. If this speculation is accurate, people should respond differently to situations framed in terms of the number of times something will happen as opposed framed in terms of the probability that something will happen.

Psychologist Paul Slovic and his colleagues presented case studies of psychiatric patients to forensic psychologists and psychiatrists about the degree of risk associated with releasing those patients into the community. The researchers framed the question differently in two conditions. In one condition, they identified the level of risk by explaining that similar people had done harm in 20 out of 100 cases; in a second condition, they stated that similar people had done harm in 20 percent of cases.

The perceived potential for harm was greater when the risk was posed in terms of number of people rather than percentage of people. The researchers suggested that with frequencies, it is easier for people to imagine what happens with 20 people, which is psychologically more real to most people than 20 percent. In both cases, the relative risk was the same. But the perceived risk was different because of the way the scenarios were framed.

The wording or the context in which **framing** occurs is an issue that can make a big difference in the way people respond to various things. In survey questions, for instance, people are more likely to agree to *assistance to the poor* than to *providing welfare*. The concept is the same in both instances, but the psychological response can differ greatly.

Confirmation Bias

When people hold beliefs, they sometimes hold those beliefs very strongly and are quite resistant to changing their minds, even in the face of evidence that contradicts those beliefs. One reason for this is **confirmation bias**. In this bias, people are more likely to seek out evidence that confirms what they believe than information that counters what they belief. The effect is further compounded by the unwillingness to accept and use new, conflicting information to adjust their beliefs. Furthermore, people tend to forget evidence that runs against what they believe. These last two points are consistent with the idea that we create schemas to help us understand the world around us; when information does not fit into a schema, it isn't clear where to put it. So we ignore it or forget it.

Overconfidence Effect

Another aspect of the unwillingness to change one's mind involves the **overconfidence effect**. People tend to have unrealistic impressions of the accuracy of their judgments. So if you ask people to give a confidence level with respect to some judgment, their stated confidence will be higher than warranted by reality. And to make matters worse, as people's confidence levels increase, so does the discrepancy between what they believe and what is true. So highly confident people tend to be highly inaccurate.

Psychological research has shown that beliefs can be hard to change, but it is not the case that people are unable or unwilling to change their minds. In this domain, as with other areas of decision making, psychologists have tended to focus on when processes break down rather than when people engage in successful behaviors.

PROBLEM SOLVING

People can be very effective at decision making; they can also fall into cognitive traps that lead to less than optimal decisions. Similarly, people can be very good at problem solving, but they can also fail to use effective strategies for problem solving. Psychologists have extensively studied the way that people solve problems and have drawn some interesting conclusions from such studies.

Psychologist Robert Sternberg, for example, has described the elements of the problem-solving cycle. These include identifying the problem, defining it, developing a strategy to solve it, organizing information about the problem, deciding how much time and effort to apply to it, monitoring progress in solving the problem, and evaluating whether one has arrived at a correct solution.

These seven elements sound daunting, but any time you have a problem to solve, like what to wear to a social gathering like a party, you engage in each of these steps. The first step in the cycle is recognizing that there is a problem to be solved. In research set up in psychological laboratories, this step is generally pretty obvious—research participants are there to solve problems that the psychologists present to them. In real life, you may not recognize that there is a problem even though you are solving problems continuously. This happens constantly and affects all of your daily activities.

In everyday life, we can solve most of our problems pretty effectively. But psychologists have devised research that tests the limits of our problem solving and how we might get stuck at any of the stages of the problem-solving cycle.

Types of Problems

Most of the problems we confront in our lives are **ill-structured problems**. They often have no single solution, and they may not have a single best solution. That is, when we solve them, we may not know if the result is the best outcome that could have occurred. For example, if you go into a large grocery store to buy a product, you may find dozens of different varieties of this specific product. Which one should you buy? There is no single answer to this question because there are different factors to consider: price, quality, brand, and so forth.

Having too much choice is not necessarily a good thing. Psychologist Barry Schwartz has studied the dynamics of having many choices and has found that too many choices can lead to indecision and lowered levels of satisfaction when a person does make a decision and picks one rather the others.

In contrast to this are **well-structured problems**. These have a clear best answer, and you can often identify a well-prescribed set of steps that you can use to solve them. Analogies are well-structured problems. Consider this example:

Sun: Solar System :: Nose:_____

(a) Smell
(b) Sneeze
(c) Face
(d) Hand

Your task in such a problem is to figure out what would correctly fill the blank. The best answer in this case would be *Face*. The logic is that the sun is at the center of the solar system, just as the nose is at the center of the face. In this problem, the task is to work with relationships among the elements of the problem.

Another type of problem requires working through a series of steps toward a specific outcome. One such problem would be to start with a word (e.g., *boat*) and then, by changing a single letter at each step, eventually create another specific new words (e.g., *sink*). There is not a single way to get from *boat* to *sink*, but the nature of the process is clearly illustrated in the following example:

BOAT
COAT
COST
CASE
BASE
BANE
BANK
SANK
SINK

There can be multiple possible paths to an answer in this type of problem, so it has more in common with everyday problems than analogies do. In a case like the word problem here, there is only one successful solution, although there are multiple paths to it. Some approaches may be better than others (such as by requiring the fewest number of steps), but you don't necessarily know if you have taken the optimal path.

Not surprisingly, there are impediments to arriving at a solution to a problem, and psychologists have discovered consistent types. We are able to solve virtually all of our problems on any given day, but once again, psychologists are interested in the process when it fails because it is in a failed situation that we can learn most about the steps people go through in problem solving and identify difficulties that people regularly encounter.

Aids to Problem Solving

When we can use what we know from previous experience to solve a new problem, it is called **positive transfer**. In some cases, prior experience blinds us to new approaches, as with fixation; such a state involves **negative transfer**.

One way to avoid negative transfer is to stop thinking about the problem for a while. Most people are familiar with the insights that sometimes pop into awareness after they have deliberately put a problem aside for a while. But what typically happens here is that the problem hasn't really been put aside. Even though people have decided not to think about the problem, it is happening outside of their awareness. Such a process is called **incubation**. It seems to work most effectively if a person is not engaged in a cognitively demanding task at the same time. That is, the brain has a limited capacity for information processing, so working on a different but difficult task while incubation is in progress might use up too much capacity and preclude or hamper incubation.

Another aspect of successful problem solving is apparent when comparing how experts and novices approach problems. One notable difference between the experts and novices is that experts spend more time in generating their representation of the problem—that is, what exactly is the problem and how is it structured? Experts are also able to draw on previous experiences to recognize the similarity between a new problem and one that they faced in the past. When they can use that prior experience to help in the novel situation, they are using positive transfer.

On the other hand, novices are likely to look at the obvious, superficial characteristics of a new situation and try to find an old problem that sort of looks like the present one. If the underlying structure of the situation is different, however, the superficial similarities will not aid in solving the problem because negative transfer is at work.

Another difference between people who have expertise and those who are just learning is that experts spend more time planning for problem solving and considering global aspects of the problem. In contrast, novices are more likely to spend their time considering smaller aspects of the problem and implementing possible steps to solutions without an overall plan.

Given these differences, it is not surprising that experts are better at estimating how difficult it will be to solve a problem. In addition, with their more effective representation of the problem in a well-developed schema, they monitor their progress more carefully than novices do.

Hindrances to Problem Solving

Sometimes people fail to solve problems because of **fixation**, which relates to focusing on some aspect of a problem that gets in the way of a successful solution. One type of fixation is **functional fixedness**, which prevents us from thinking of alternative and unusual uses for common objects. A classic problem involves this situation: You want to get some light in a room without any windows. You have a candle, a box of matches, and some thumb tacks. How could you mount a candle on the wall so that it does not drip wax on the floor when you light it?

This problem is hard to solve because it involves using one of the objects in an unusual way. The solution is to empty the box of matches and tack the empty box onto the wall. You can then put the candle in the matchbox so that when you light it, the wax does not drip onto the floor. The mental set that poses the problem in this situation is that people regard a matchbox as a container for holding matches, not as a candle holder. It can be difficult to overcome this mindset.

Using these three objects, how can you affix the candle to the wall so that the candle does not drip wax onto the floor when lit? *(Shutterstock)*

Another type of hindrance involves **mental set**. Sometimes we develop strategies for successful problem solving, but when we are in a new situation, those old strategies may not work. For instance, if you bought a new cell phone, it would not be unusual to follow a set of steps that worked on your old phone to try to set the same application on the new one. Unfortunately, the new phone requires a different setup and it may be hard to figure out that a different series of steps is needed.

Another deterrent to problem solving is the imposition of **unnecessary constraints**. In more familiar terms this simply means that people sometimes fail to think "outside the box." They worry that they cannot take certain steps to solve a problem, without considering that they can probably approach the problem from a different direction. The well-known Nine-Dot Problem (see Figure 2.2) illustrates how people fail to recognize unusual strategies.

One solution to this problem appears in Figure 2.3. Some people feel that this solution is cheating, but the directions say nothing about staying within the imagined box in which people see the dots. There is no box, and there is no rule that says that you cannot draw lines outside of the imaginary box.

Yet another barrier to successful problem solving involves focusing on irrelevant information. Sometimes a solution is simpler than we might imagine. Imagine a real-life situation in which you had to solve some problem. If you looked around you, you would have seen many objects that would not be at all useful for this objective. So you ignored them. In some cases, however, people have a difficult time separating useful and useless objects. This has been observed in laboratory studies that psychologists have devised to study problem-solving techniques and processes. Although most of the objects or elements/objects they make available to participants are part of the solution,

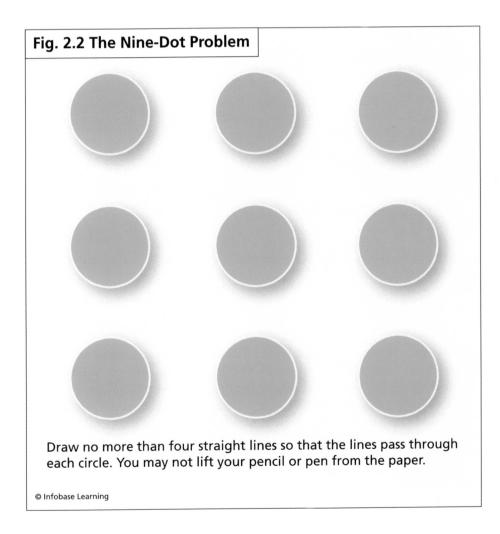

Fig. 2.2 The Nine-Dot Problem

Draw no more than four straight lines so that the lines pass through each circle. You may not lift your pencil or pen from the paper.

© Infobase Learning

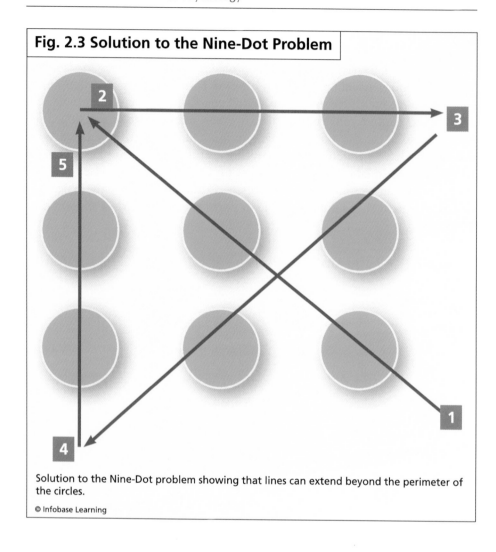

Fig. 2.3 Solution to the Nine-Dot Problem

Solution to the Nine-Dot problem showing that lines can extend beyond the perimeter of the circles.

© Infobase Learning

psychologists throw in an additional, totally useless object to see whether participants can distinguish relevant from irrelevant parts of the solution and whether the useless objects are ignored or become a distraction.

To illustrate this more clearly we can revisit the problem dealing with affixing a candle to a wall so that it illuminated the room but did not drip on the floor. Everything in the description of the problem was part of the solution. The simple solution to this problem was to use the matchbox as a candle holder. Now suppose that you had learned there was a fourth object—a newspaper—in addition to the matchbox with matches, the thumb tacks, and the candle. You might have tried to fit the newspaper into your solution when, in fact, the paper would have been entirely unnecessary and would have distracted you from

Creativity Is Not an Accident

Some people seem to have a knack of coming up with witty responses in social situations. Others can combine an unusual set of ingredients to produce an interesting and delicious meal. Still others, when faced with an emergency, can create a useful tool from unrelated parts. All of these people could be said to have one particular characteristic in common: They are creative.

Psychologists identify **creativity** as the production of something that is original and valuable. (In this case, *valuable* does not necessarily mean worth money, although that is not out of the question. Here we are talking about something that others appreciate.) People think of artists and musicians as being creative, but it is clear that people can be creative in areas other than the arts. In fact, psychologists have begun to recognize the importance of studying everyday creativity.

Creative people are generally above average in intelligence, although beyond a certain level (an IQ of 120 or so), increases in intelligence do not signal increases in creativity. So to be creative, you need to have a certain degree of intelligence, but you do not have to be a genius. In fact, different areas of the brain seem to be involved in intelligence (the parietal lobe) versus creativity (the frontal lobe). Keep in mind, though, that for most cognitive tasks, it is not correct to say that there is a single area of the brain involved in the tasks; thought is a process that integrates input from diverse areas of the brain.

Robert Sternberg has outlined five general characteristics of people who are creative. First, they have an area of expertise. It is unlikely that somebody is going to show creativity in an area simply by accident. Rather, people typically spend a lot of time, energy, and thought to develop expertise before they are able to show creativity in a given area.

Second, creativity requires that people be able to think imaginatively. That is, a person needs the skill to take two (or more) unrelated ideas and combine them in a novel way. For example, the famous psychologist B.F. Skinner developed some of his research in operant conditioning after a Skinner box malfunctioned one night and he noted an interesting pattern of behavior by the animal in the operant chamber.

A third characteristic of creativity is a personality that tolerates ambiguity and will continue working toward a goal in spite of initial setbacks. As a rule, an innovator is likely to experience many failures on the route to success. Or as Thomas Edison is reputed to have said, "Genius is one percent inspiration and ninety-nine percent perspiration."

Another aspect of creativity is that it requires intrinsic motivation. People can make a lot of money from innovative and creative products, but research

(continues)

(continued)

has shown that it is not the monetary payoff that motivates them. Rather, they thrive on the challenge of the project itself. Based on what we know about the overjustification effect, if a person concentrates too much on external rewards, the motivation for pursuing a difficult task may diminish.

Finally, creativity is more likely to emerge when a person is laboring in an environment that values it. As such, creativity arises when people are helped by others to reach their goals. The idea of a single person working alone to come up with an idea is generally misplaced. Creativity arises within a social context because, no matter how novel an idea, it will have arisen from some combination of other ideas.

So if you want to be creative, you should be prepared to learn the fundamentals of the area you are working with, to think outside the box, to experience multiple failures before you succeed, to be vitally interested in the idea for its own sake, and to choose an environment in which you receive support. Creativity is not an end point. It is a process.

solving the problem. One important aspect of problem solving is to recognize what information is useful and what information is either irrelevant or a hindrance.

The final type of hindrance that we will discuss here is confirmation bias. This may be most relevant when we try to evaluate whether we are making progress toward solving a problem or have solved it successfully. One way to see if you have solved the problem is to see if your solution holds up when you test it.

In many cases, people do not do a good job of testing their solution. They work to confirm it when they should be trying to make it fail. It may seem counterintuitive to want to generate a failure when you test for a successful solution, but that is the only way to discover if there are problems.

CONCLUSION

We make decisions and solve problems every day of our lives. Most of the time, we don't think of our lives as being filled with such decisions because we arrive at those decisions and make judgments quickly and easily most of the time. Nonetheless, each time we arrive at some conclusion, it is the result of a number of steps that begin with a problem and end with a solution.

Psychologists have identified the steps we go through during problem solving, from recognizing that there is a problem to be solved through evaluating whether we have reached a successful end point. At any stage of the process, there are ways that our decisions might be helped or hindered. In psychological research, investigators have broken down the process so we can determine what kinds of errors are common in various situations.

Further Reading

Myers, David G. *Intuition: Its Powers and Perils*. New Haven, Conn: Yale University Press. 2004.

Stanovich, Keith E. *How to Think Straight About Psychology*. 7th ed. Boston, Mass.: Allyn & Bacon, 2004.

Tavris, Carol. *Psychobabble and Biobunk. Using Psychological Science to Think Critically About Popular Psychology*. 3rd ed. Boston, Mass.: Prentice Hall, 2011.

CHAPTER 3

LANGUAGE

Humans are able to communicate about things that haven't happened, things that may never happen, and things that have happened in the past. This one unique skill, our ability to communicate complex ideas through language, completely separates people from all other creatures.

One remarkable aspect of this uniquely human ability is its versatility. We use language in everyday conversation, to convey our innermost thoughts, to talk about things that matter to us, to tell jokes, to make plans, etc. And in today's world, we also use language as a means of trying to pass information on from one person to another in a variety of different formats.

One example of this is texting, a very convenient, very common method of communication among people in the United States. Using new technology and our fingers we can communicate a great number of ideas; for many students, texting has become the primary means of communicating with friends and even parents. As the technology continues to evolve, the format and process will become more sophisticated, as will new conventions on texting.

Other, more traditional means include face-to-face speech, the written word, and the telephone. But no matter the form, language is a tool we use to communicate socially, to pass along information, to share ideas and thoughts and emotions. This chapter examines several different aspects of this wonderful skill and how psychologists study this uniquely human behavior.

WHAT IS LANGUAGE?

One of the principal questions that psychologists have asked about language is "What exactly is it?" This is a question compounded by the fact that we aren't even sure how many languages exist in today's world. Most people, if they even bothered to think about this question, would have their own ideas about the nature of language and what it is; the answers would vary widely.

Scientifically defined, language is a complex communication system that involves the use of abstract symbols to convey virtually unlimited messages. It is typically spoken, but there are other forms that rely on a variety of processes by which language can be conveyed (writing and reading, sign language, etc.). If we follow that definition closely, we must eliminate animal communication because there are limits to how and what animals can communicate. For example, birds can use birdsong to attract a mate, but the birdsong does not allow for the variety of information associated with human communication. Birdsong merely conveys an immediate need; human language, in its infinite variety, does much more.

Human language, for example, can express meaning about events or ideas that have not yet happened, things that happened in the past, and things that may never happen. Because our language can transcend time and space, we have an unlimited ability to communicate ideas. This is not a minor point. Neither is the idea only humans can fully understand, produce, or reproduce human language. Although some would argue that the differences between animal communication and human language can be a very fine line, a great deal of research that has led to the conclusion that most animals do not possess the vocal apparatus to produce speech, and no animals have the brain capacity to produce the complex language that humans produce. There is evidence that some animals can understand human speech, but there is no evidence to date that animals can actually produce language, even at the level of a human two year old.

The discussion on how animal communication differs from human language is not presented here as a matter of peripheral interest. Instead, it is critically important to understanding the question of what language is and what language is not. Part of this understanding relies on knowing what separates language from other forms of communication Another important component to understanding human language is that it is universal, that is, people all over the world use language. There are, according to current estimates, approximately 4,000 known spoken languages. Each of these is a system that allows for rich communication, but each has different methods and features. And this underscores another important fact about language, the fact that it is extremely flexible.

The concepts of flexibility and universality will be discussed later in this chapter. Here the focus returns to differentiating human language from animal communication, arguably the cornerstone of the definition of language.

Animal Studies

Over the years, researchers have designed numerous animal studies to test whether animals could develop language. The goals have always been to provide direct evidence that, under the right circumstances, animals could produce language in the same manner as humans. Much in the same way scientists have spent time working on developing computers that can think, psychologists have devoted entire careers to working with animals, attempting to demonstrate that animals have the capability of sustained human-like communication and that this ability simply needs to be further developed.

The most famous of these studies were conducted with chimpanzees, including **Washoe**, who was trained by psychologists Beatrix and Allen Gardner; **Nim Chimpsky**, trained by Herb Terrace; and a bonobo (pygmy chimpanzee) named **Kanzi**, trained by Sue Savage-Rumbaugh. All of these animals experienced optimal training situations. In each case, the animals were brought into a lab and provided with a highly structured, very rich environment with carefully designed training procedures. All the animals developed a relatively high degree of language comprehension skills, although these skills did not develop spontaneously and required intensive training.

The trainers used a variety of different techniques. The Gardners, for example, taught Washoe American Sign Language. After years of working with Washoe, they argued that she showed remarkable comprehension and was able to produce hundreds of independent signs. Based on video and written evidence, it appeared that Washoe did develop a large repertoire of signs that allowed her to produce a great number of unique, language-like utterances. Moreover, Washoe could sign information and gesture enough to convey meaning covering a wide range of topics and issues. She even signed with other chimps as a means of communication. Based on these achievements, the Gardners argued that Wahoe demonstrated that a chimp reared as a human can develop many skills that a human child would develop, including a system that allows for communication with the trainers.

Herb Terrace's chimp Nim was brought each day to the lab to be trained in human communication systems, similar to the way Washoe was trained. However, Terrace's goal was to see if the chimp could produce sentences that would show maturity in language development. That never happened, and Terrace concluded that chimps could never produce human-like language.

As a result of his studies, Terrace could not agree with the Gardners' conclusions and generated a structured rebuttal against the work they had published. He argued that after years of training Nim, the animal was unable to master at a comparable level the repertoire of signs and abilities that the Gardners claimed to have developed in Washoe. According to Terrace, the Gardners' videos contained evidence that Washoe was, in fact, coached to answer questions correctly. The Gardners countered that the goals of the two studies were

Kanzi, the Pygmy Chimpanzee

Kanzi is a 30 year old bonobo (pygmy) chimpanzee who currently resides in Iowa at the Great Ape Conservatory. His trainer, Sue Savage-Rumbaugh, has been working with Kanzi for approximately 25 years, and in that time, he has developed what has been reported to be an amazing ability to deal with all aspects of human language, albeit through a message board of lexigrams rather than through human speech.

The research on Kanzi is really quite compelling. It started with Kanzi's adopted mother, Matata (an aggressive female bonobo) claiming Kanzi as her own. When Matata was brought to the Language Research Lab in Georgia, Kanzi accompanied her. The original research involved Matata; Savage-Rumbaugh and her colleague, Duane Rumbaugh, were trying to teach Matata to use the lexigram board to convey messages. Matata did not seem to grasp the possibilities of the board and did not use it except when directed to by the researchers. Kanzi, however, did grasp the potential and began to use the board without prompting. Over time, Kanzi began to use the lexigram board more and more and after several years, began showing remarkable language skills.

Kanzi is very good at understanding what is said to him, as evidenced by the fact that when given directions, he can follow them easily and demonstrate

very different, and that the attack on their work was unwarranted. According to the Gardners, the goal of their research was simply to demonstrate that in an enriched environment, an animal can learn to communicate using a human-developed system. The debate over the language abilities of animals raged on over the next several years, with the researchers on both sides producing volumes of results that are still somewhat ambiguous.

In a different set of animal studies, Sue Savage-Rumbaugh spent decades working with a bonobo chimpanzee named Kanzi. Kanzi learned how to communicate via a message board rather than learning American Sign Language. The story of Savage-Rumbaugh's experiences with Kanzi is very interesting and is highlighted in the sidebar above.

Research on a different type of animal has also shed light on the controversy regarding language in nonhuman animals. One case that garnered a great deal of attention over the years is that of **Alex the Parrot**, a grey African Parrot that was heralded as a prodigy. A video of Alex demonstrated an animal that seemed to have the ability to speak in simple, short sentences, and even understand complex questions and requests. In a typical conversation (part of the video) Alex was asked if he could tell which of two different colored keys was bigger. Alex would respond with the correct answer, naming the color of the correct key.

behaviorally that he has comprehended what was asked of him. However, the results are not as promising when it comes to language production: The bottom line is that Kanzi cannot produce sentences nearly as well as he can understand them. Evidence suggests, however, that he can produce unique utterances (even in combination) and is able to communicate ideas in a way that is understandable to others besides his trainers.

But has Kanzi learned language? Before we draw the conclusion that the skills that Kanzi possesses are language, it's important to note that he did not develop these skills intuitively and semi-independently, that is, in the manner that humans do. Kanzi required an enormous amount of work with his trainer to hone and utilize these skills. Over time, these skills improved, but they were still only as good as the skills typical mastered by young children. Specifically, with 25 years of training in an enriched, verbal environment, Kanzi was only able to produce language at the level of a 2 or 3 year old human child. That relatively low level of functioning suggests that although we might be able to get animals to develop linguistic skills that might be similar to human linguistic skills if we train them long enough and hard enough, the divide between human language and pseudo-language is still quite large.

Demonstrations such as these help convinced some people that human language is not as unique to our species as we like to think that it is. But many critics continue to argue that such research proves very little. In the case of Alex, for example, critics cite a problem with the method of communication, a frequently contested issue. With most animal studies, the trainers use some form of communication that requires an alternative method of sharing ideas (e.g., gesturing, message boards, etc.), none of which can actually be called "language." The reason for this alternative is the rather simple fact that most animals don't have the physical ability to produce human speech sounds.

Alex, however, was a parrot, and as we know, parrots do have the ability to vocalize. In fact, parrots are very, very good at imitating sounds that they hear. With extensive training, parrots can talk. The typical parrot will say things relating to food or some other oft repeated phrase—and this happens not only in a research laboratory but even in private homes.

What made Alex unique was not his ability to vocalize words, but rather his ability to vocalize words in the appropriate context in response to a question. By responding with color words to indicate his understanding of different-sized keys, Alex showed he could understand the question. He could also choose

Alex the Parrot, who learned to respond appropriately to verbal commands. *(Photo by Michael Goldman/Time Life Pictures/Getty)*

an object based on an understanding subtle, distinguishing features (size and color). Thus, according to many scientists, Alex had developed the ability for language.

The overarching question here concerns the issue of language production. That is, did Alex ever produce novel language? The answer is no. Alex could respond to questions posed to him, but he couldn't really formulate unique, novel sentences. What made Alex unique was that he was trained with a great deal of patience over a long period of time so that his interactions with humans was much more human-like than was the behavior of other animals. However, left alone, and without the intensive human interaction, Alex would not have developed the skills that he so deftly portrayed.

Although the details of these studies are not that important for our discussion here, the impression that they give is that language is a uniquely human activity. None of the animals described above would have developed language on their own. These animals were given all the chances to learn how to produce language, and they were unable to develop the ability to generate complex aspects of language that humans take for granted. They produced "words," but they didn't produce language the way humans do.

STRUCTURE OF SPOKEN LANGUAGE
Phonemes
According to many linguists and psycholinguists (psychologists who study language), language is a multilayered process. The description of how the process works typically starts with the concept of phonemes. A **phoneme** represents the smallest unit of sound in a particular language. For example, all the letters of the alphabet we use are phonemes (although there is some overlap; for example, *c* can make the *k* or the *s* sound).

In English, we produce all the unique sounds that we are able to make by combining only about 40 to 50 unique phonemes. These sounds can be combined in an infinite number of ways to produce the rich number of sounds possible in our language. (Other languages make do with fewer phonemes; some languages have more. For example, Polynesian languages use about 15 phonemes, whereas some African languages may have 100.)

An interesting fact is that the phonemes differ by region of the country. In the Northeast (Massachusetts, in particular) there are accents that change the sounds of some phonemes. These changes don't render those sounds meaningless to those who aren't from the Northeast, but make them sound different to people who don't live in that region of the country. In the South, the sounds are often elongated, a process that gives rise to what we call "the Southern accent." These minor changes do not cause big problems with native speakers of English, but non-native speakers often struggle with them.

Morphemes

The second level of language is the **morpheme**, which, according to linguists is the smallest unit of meaning in a language. So, small words, such as *cat* or *walk* contain only one morpheme. If we add the letter *s* to *cat* to make *cats*, we have a word with two morphemes (cat) and (s); if we add *ing* to *walk*, we also have a word with two morphemes (walk) and (ing). These simple examples, but several

Regional Accents in the United States— What Do You Sound Like?

One of the more interesting aspects of English in the United States is that depending on where you are in the country, English can sound different. In parts of Massachusetts, speakers will often drop the /r/ sound at the end of a word and replace it with an /ah/. So, *car* because *cah*, and *far* becomes *fah*. Moreover, words in this region of the country (the Northeast) tend to be spoken more quickly than in other parts of the country. Words also tend to be shortened and clipped so that *something* becomes *somthin* and *everybody* becomes *evybudy*. To the untrained listener not previously exposed to this accent, it sounds awkward. And, when people try to fake the accent, the results sound less than authentic.

In other parts of the country, the accent is very different. In the mid-Atlantic states, there is a tendency to add the /r/ sound to words that don't have them. For example, *wash* becomes *warsh*, and *water* becomes *warter*. These accents are learned the same way any other part of language is learned. Thus, they are not a sign of anything other than where the person was raised and what kind of accent the person heard while growing up.

What's interesting about these accents is their origin. In many ways, all regional accents have a long history based on who settled a given area and how long those people stayed there. In the Northeast, and Massachusetts in general, there is a trace of British in the accent that can be linked to the strong and lengthy British presence in the area. Although the U.S. population is quite transient (i.e., people move all over the place), there are enough native speakers in the Northeast who were raised with this accent to make it essentially a "mother tongue" for this region.

It would be interesting to see how regional accents change or don't change over the next 200 years. Will the accents familiar to us remain the same, fade out entirely or take on new nuances introduced by our transient society or even globalization? Although we will have to wait for the answer, it is certain that languages will likely evolve and speech sounds will change.

different morphemes can also be combined to produce longer and more complex words, each having a unique meaning.

Native English speakers know this intuitively and regard it as natural. But not all languages share this structure. For example, Chinese is a tonal language that relies on changing intonation in words for meaning, so Chinese morphemes are much different from English morphemes, both in written and in spoken language. The basic sound for *ma*, for example, can be pronounced several different ways in Chinese, depending on the intended meaning. If the tone rises on the vowel, it means one thing; if the tone falls on the vowel, it means something else. The difference is also expressed in the written characters for *ma*, which reflect both the differences in intonation and in meaning.

The way native speakers of tonal languages learn to speak is no different than the way anyone else learns to speak. They just learn to attend to different aspects of speech to determine the intent of the speaker.

Syntax

The next level of language is the syntactic level. To many, this is considered to be one of the most important aspects of language. **Syntax** refers to word order and sentence structure. Typically in English, we place nouns or subjects first and verbs or predicates second. We can reverse the order, but we do so only in specific situations. One example is how we can turn a declarative sentence into a question by inverting the order of a verb and a noun: Thus *John went to the store to buy milk.* becomes *Did John go to the store to buy milk?* In some languages, the meaning of a sentence can also be changed by intonation. In Spanish (and in English, for that matter), you can change a statement into a question by changing the way you inflect the final word of the sentence. With a flat tone, the sentence is a declarative sentence. With a rising tone, it's a question. Indeed, all languages are full of rich examples of different structures that alter meaning, provide emphasis, or produce other interesting effects.

In English, we often interpret the meaning of a word or the part of speech of a word by its placement in a sentence. For example, if a word follows the word *the*, it has to be a noun, an adjective, or an adverb. That is, you would not place the word *the* before a verb. If you did, a listener would interpret that word as a noun rather than a verb, regardless of the intention of the speaker. In fact, we often use this fact to help us understand words that we do not understand. The ability to disambiguate words that we don't know is critical in understanding language; we are able to do this with the speed and efficiency that we take for granted because we can anticipate the nature of the words we are going to hear.

Suppose you hear a new word, *plambe*. That word could mean anything. However, if I put it in a sentence, such as *I had to plambe at school today*, you now know that *plambe* is a verb. And you now do certain things with this word based on its usage. You could say, for example, *Yesterday, I plambed* or *Tomorrow, I will plambe.* By understanding that my word placement dictates that *plambe* is a verb, you would able to apply the rules that you have learned to that word and use that word correctly in a sentence even without knowing what the word actually means. The same holds true if I tell you that *I found a godger yesterday in my back yard.* You might ask, *Only one godger or two godgers?* showing that you understand the rules of pluralization.

HOW DO WE LEARN LANGUAGE?

Within the broad community of psychologists, language learning is an issue rife with controversy. The behavioral school suggests that we learn language according to the same principles that we learn any other behavior. We are exposed to things in the environment and, if they are reinforced, the probability of the behavior being performed again increases.

Rules of Grammar and Origins of English

It often seems as though the rules of language have been simply handed down to us from generation to generation with a few mild alterations along the way. In fact, nothing could be further from the truth. It is true that English, as we know it, is similar (though not identical) to English as it was spoken 100 years ago. However, today's English sounds nothing like the English of 500 years ago or even 300 years ago. What has happened is that English has changed, evolved, and become a very different language. One of the more important changes that has occurred involves the rules of the language.

English emerged from necessity. Before there was English, the native language of England was Celtic. Over the centuries, England was attacked and invaded by people who did not speak Celtic and brought their own languages to the lands they attacked and invaded. Celtic had to be modified so the natives of England could communicate with those who had invaded. An interesting side note to this can be seen in the English that came into use after the Norman invasion of 1066. Consider, for example, that animal names like *swine, deer,* and *cow* derive from Old or Middle English, whereas *pork, venison,* and *beef* come from French; this may reflect the respective roles of the native people who raised the animals and the French invaders who ate them.

But the language-blending phenomenon had begun long before the French arrived, and some of the most interesting changes can be seen in the poetic works of various eras. As "English" took on characteristics of many different languages (Anglo-Saxon, German, Celtic), what emerged was what we now call Old English, a language that didn't look anything like our modern version

The learning theorists (such as Skinner) have argued that we learn how to produce and use language over the course of several years through various forms of reinforcement. We are exposed to language, we learn how to control our tongue and lips so we can produce sounds, and we learn that certain sounds result in certain reinforcers. We repeat those sounds and eventually, we couple sounds into phrases, sentences, etc. Through such a process, we learn all of our vocabulary, our ability to determine parts of speech, and the sounds that are associated with many of the sounds in our native language. We also learn to stop producing sounds that are no longer appropriate for the language that we speak.

Nativists (such as Chomsky) have argued that we are "hard wired" to learn language, and that humans are unique in this respect. According to a nativist perspective, there is something unique about the human brain that is designed to learn and use language in ways no other organism can. This argument stems

of English at all. Consider the following sentence from *Beowulf*: "Þæt wæs god cyning!" This translates, roughly, to "That was a good king!" As you can see, Old English contains characters and spelling that we don't use anymore.

Middle English, although not nearly as different from modern English as Old English was, also produced numerous changes in spelling and grammar rules. Consider the following excerpt from *Canterbury Tales* of English poet Geoffrey Chaucer: "Whan *that Aueryłł* wt his shoures soote," which translates to "When April with his sweet showers." Again, there are spelling differences and differences in letters used, but as you can see, as the language changes, it begins to look more and more like Modern English.

Another change was the transition from using *–en* to pluralize nouns to using *–s*. This change occurred between Middle English and the English of Shakespeare. In fact, today, there are still two words that consistently utilize the *–en* strategy (*children* and *oxen*). In other cases, the *–en* has almost vanished but can still be heard or read occasionally For example, *brother* was once pluralized as *brethren*, but is now almost always pluralized as *brothers*. Both versions are acceptable.

This change in the construction of plural nouns occurred for no really good reason, much in the same way that the meanings of many words change for no really good reason. A contemporary example of such changes is the odd construction that is used so often in high schools around the country, where students have started dropping the definite article (*the*) or the indefinite article (*a*) before the word "prom" and have changed "Rob invited me to the prom" or "Rob invited me to a prom" to "Rob invited me to prom." There is no known reason for this change. It happened and it seems to have taken root.

from the fact that we don't have to have to teach children language, yet all children learn it at about the same rate, as shown in Table 3.1.

Each theory on language learning has its ardent supporters. Most recently, however, psychological discussions on language learning favor a cognitive approach over a behavioral approach.

The pattern outlined in Table 3.1 is predictable not only in English. Other languages show the same pattern of language acquisition. Even with obvious differences in languages, the ability to produce sounds, to construct sentences, and to convey meaning follows the same pattern in all humans.

In addition, children seem to make the same predictions about language usage at about the same time. For example, if English-speaking children are told that they are looking a *wug* and are then asked what one would say if there were two of these critters, they will say *wugs*. And if they are told that a person will *wick*, they will generate the forms *wicked* and *wicking,* a rather clear indication that they seem to be learning rules that they can then apply where appropriate.

LINGUISTIC UNIVERSALS

According to the work of the linguist Charles Hockett, all typically developing children learn language in a predictable way; furthermore, he contended, all languages across cultures have characteristics in common. The flavor of these **linguistic universals** is important for understanding the unique properties

TABLE 3.1
Typical Milestones in the Development of Language

Age	Milestone
Birth to 2 months	Cooing
2 months to 12 months	Babbling
Approximately 12 months	First word (typically a simple sound such as "da")
Approximately 16 months	Two word utterances
2 to 6 years of age	Add 6 to 10 new words per day; overextension (doggie for every four-legged animal)
Age 5	Over regularization: "I goed to the store."
From age 5 on	Add words to vocabulary; learn subtleties of language

Everybody Spoke Sign Language

In the first few centuries of the European occupation of Martha's Vineyard in Massachusetts, there was a high rate of deafness among people there. About 10 percent of the population was deaf. The deafness resulted from the genetic heritage of original settlers from one locale in England.

The culture of the community was that deafness was not a disability. Rather, it was simply a trait that some people showed. The effect was that everybody in that community used sign language. People who could hear also spoke, of course. But nobody was excluded from participation in the community because of deafness.

Elsewhere, such acceptance was far from the norm. In most places, people who could not hear were excluded from social life and had little or no educational opportunity. In some religious circles, they were not considered fully human because they did not have aural language.

Newcomers to the island sometimes inquired whether people who were deaf were allowed to participate in civic life; for people arriving there from the mainland, deafness was a disability that led to exclusion in their world. But for residents of the island, this question made no sense whatsoever. In contrast to the situation on the mainland, deaf people on Martha's Vineyard were among the most educated people in the community. They often traveled off the island to receive an education. So when they returned, they often held important positions.

At one point, an off-islander asked if there were any mentally retarded people on the island. A resident named several people, but it turned out to be a hoax. Later, the off-islander discovered that the resident had named the only Democrats on the island.

of human language; we will present three important characteristics of these universals.

First, language shows **arbitrariness**. That means that words are not inherently imbued with meaning. Rather, words are selected to stand for objects in the world in an arbitrary manner. *Dog* in English is *chien* in French. The only difference is that speakers of English have agreed to call canines *dogs*, whereas speakers of French have agreed to call these animals *chien*.

Second, language involves **displacement**. Language allows us to talk about events that have already happened, events that will happen, and events that may never happen at all. No other form of communication allows for this.

Third, language involves a **vocal-auditory channel**. Languages in all cultures rely on the vocal auditory channel as the primary form of communication using language. Other manifestations of language, such as sign language, involve nonvocal communication, though, so the so-called universality of the vocal-auditory channel is not really universal.

Hockett named other linguistic universals, but this list represents some of the most important for distinguishing between human language and other forms of communication.

CONCLUSION

Language is a concept that many psychologists have investigated extensively. It is one of the characteristics that make humans unique among animals. Although there is controversy over how we learn it, we know that it is learned in a predictable pattern that is consistent across cultures and languages.

Language helps us understand cognition more effectively because it is the gateway to the cognitive system. Through the study of language, we have access to the organization of memory and the skills and strategies humans use to solve problems. In other chapters of this book, you will see information that highlights how language allows us to view and study the internal workings of the human information processing system.

Further Reading

Groce, Nora Ellen. *Everyone Here Spoke Sign Language.* Cambridge, Mass: Harvard University Press, 1985.

Pinker, Steven. *The Language Instinct: How the Mind Creates Language.* New York, NY: Perennial Press, 2000.

CHAPTER 4

INTELLIGENCE

WHAT IS INTELLIGENCE?

Is it possible to measure something if we don't really know what it is? Although this sounds like a strange question, it is one that psychologists have had to address for the past century. In fact, some of the most important work that psychologists engage in is endeavoring to assess very complex, internal concepts that we cannot directly observe.

One of these concepts is **intelligence**, which psychologists study as a means of understanding human thought and behavior. One seemingly obvious characteristic of intelligence is that (as a rule) people with more intelligence do things better than people with less intelligence. But even though it is relatively easy to see this idea at work, we still don't really know what intelligence is.

What we do know (or at least think we know) is that the degree or level of intelligence a person has makes a difference in behavior, and it is this understanding that prompts us to study intelligence. At the same time, we are limited to direct observations of the effects of intelligence, not observations of intelligence itself. In scientific parlance, we refer to this as a **hypothetical construct**, that is an idea that we think is useful but that we cannot actually see.

Psychology is not the only science that relies on hypothetical constructs. Physics is often approached the same way. In considering gravity, for example, physicists know that it is a useful concept because it relates to and affects things that occur in the physical world. We all know that if you drop something, it falls down rather than up, and that's because of gravity. But what we actually see is not gravity itself but the effects of gravity. So physicists measure the effects of gravity even though they cannot see gravity itself just as psychologists measure the effects of intelligence even though they cannot see intelligence.

EARLY ATTEMPTS TO MEASURE INTELLIGENCE

The first scientific attempts to measure intelligence were based on the evolutionary theory proposed by Charles Darwin, and the person associated with these initial attempts was psychologist James McKeen Cattell. Cattell's first attempts at measuring intelligence were not particularly useful, but they opened the door to a new and exciting field of study. Cattell coined the term **mental test** in the 1890s, and generations of psychologists have been devising their own measuring instruments and trying to measure intelligence in meaningful ways since that time.

Cattell's work in studying intelligence focused on sensory measurements, which from a contemporary perspective seems like a strange way to measure intelligence. At the time, however, the prevailing scientific logic was that all information from the world around us entered the brain through the senses. Consequently, people with more highly evolved brains (i.e., more intelligent people) should have better sensory functioning.

Cattell developed a total of 50 measurements that relied on seeing, hearing, touch, motor movement, estimates of time, and judgments of intensity of stimuli. As we will see, these measurements are generally absent from the widely used intelligence tests of our time.

Clark Wissler, one of Cattell's students, conducted research to validate Cattell's measurements of intelligence. The results of Wissler's work were very disappointing to Cattell. The measurements on the various tests should have correlated. If they all measured intelligence or mental acuity, a person who scored well on one should score well on the others. Unfortunately, the results showed no relationship among the variables. This led Wissler, and other psychologists, to abandon Cattell's approach.

Alfred Binet and Théodore Simon subsequently developed a set of educationally related measurements that led to modern models of intelligence tests. Binet and Simon used their test to determine if children in Paris schools were performing at low levels and would benefit from special educational interventions.

The intent behind the research conducted by Binet and Simon was purely practical. They had an educational question to answer, and the test they had designed answered the question. An American psychologist named Henry Goddard translated their test into English in 1910. In 1916, the revised version was translated by Lewis Terman at Stanford University and renamed the Stanford Revision of the Binet-Simon Scale. Robert Yerkes, then president of the American Psychological Association, used Terman's test during World War I to measure the intelligence of thousands of soldiers in the U.S. military, thus conducting the first intelligence test ever administered on such a wide scale.

James McKeen Cattell, American psychologist who coined the term mental test. *(Wikipedia)*

The Initial Attempt to Measure Mental Processes

James McKeen Cattell believed that he could determine a person's intelligence level by measuring how efficient that person's sensory processing was. He proposed that psychologists conduct research that was based on this theory to identify the best ways to assess mental processes. Cattell's ten initial test items are presented below:

- How much pressure a person could generate by squeezing the hand
- How quickly a person could move the arm 50 centimeters (about 20 inches)
- The distance that two pointed implements must be separated on the skin for a person to feel that there are two rather than one
- The degree of pressure needed to cause pain
- The smallest difference in the weight of two objects needed for a person to detect that they are different
- The reaction time for sound
- The time needed to name colors
- How accurately a person could bisect a 50 centimeter line
- How accurately a person could indicate a 10-second time interval
- Number of letters remembered when presented at a rate of two per second

Cattell administered these tests to people who came to his laboratory and reserved 40 additional measurement items for students in his laboratory. He recommended a systematic investigation of these measurements to establish standardized norms.

Although his tests proved to be unsuitable for assessing intelligence, his ideas paved the way for more refined and useful measurements.

It was not long before psychologists and others began to regard the Stanford-Binet as a general test of intelligence, even though its origin was as an educational measurement. Even today, intelligence tests include items relevant to tasks associated with learning.

Psychologist David Wechsler later developed tests that still exist in revised form today, the Wechsler Adult Intelligence Scale (WAIS) and the Wechsler Intelligence Scale for Children (WISC). Wechsler's first test appeared in 1939. The Stanford-Binet test dominated the testing world until the 1960s, when psychologists and others determined that the Wechsler test (and particularly its subtests) had certain advantages that permitted assessment of a broader range of mental abilities.

THEORETICAL APPROACHES TO UNDERSTANDING INTELLIGENCE

James McKeen Cattell's approach to mental testing was based on evolutionary theory, and based on this theory, the connection he drew between sensory performance and intelligence was logical. Unfortunately, this theoretical model of intelligence did not provide any real insights into human intelligence. Subsequently, other psychologists have proposed models of intelligence based on empirical data rather than existing theory. These models use what is known as a **psychometric approach** that relies on statistical analyses of the relationships among various measurements of intelligence. The models have taken various forms. Some suggest that intelligence exists as a single element; others posit that intelligence has multiple components.

British psychologist Charles Spearman proposed an early model of intelligence in 1904 that survives to this day. He believed that intelligence consisted of a single fundamental element, usually referred to simply as the g-**factor**, because it referred to a general aspect of intelligence. Even though he argued for a single aspect of intelligence, Spearman also recognized that there were more specific kinds of abilities that were important in understanding intelligence. He referred to these specific subfactors as s-**factors**.

Researchers regularly find that the subfactors of intelligence correlate with one another. This finding suggests that the subfactors themselves are not independent of one another, so it is reasonable to conclude that they might be influenced by g, a person's general level of intelligence.

Contrasting with Spearman's theory, the multifactor approach of American psychologist Joy Paul Guilford speculated that intelligence consisted of three major dimensions, each of which had subcomponents. The operations dimension related to areas like memory and divergent thinking; the information dimension related to types of processing, like visual and auditory; the product dimension related to how the other dimensions are used, as in identifying relationships among ideas.

Guilford initially posited that intelligence consisted of 120 components when the various dimensions with their subfactors are combined. He later elaborated on the model and generated 180 components. Psychologists today do not regard Guilford's model as valid, although there are current theories that do include more than a single g-factor such as the one that Spearman identified.

The most current psychometric approach to measuring intelligence is based on work by Raymond Cattell, John Horn, and John Carroll, and is known as the Cattell-Horn-Carroll (CHC) theory of cognitive abilities. This theory suggests that there are broad and narrow levels of ability. The ten broad levels appear in Table 4.1.

RELIABIABILITY AND VALIDITY OF IQ SCORES

Research has documented the reliability of measures of intelligence. In this sense, reliability refers to the degree to which a person will obtain similar scores either when retaking the same test or generating similar scores on different tests that purport to measure the same thing. In general, the reliability of tests is quite good. The correlation between scores in retesting is .90 or higher, with a perfect correlation being 1.00.

TABLE 4.1

The Ten Broad Stratum Abilities of the Cattell-Horn-Carroll Theory of Cognitive Abilities

Ability	Nature of the Ability
Crystallized intelligence	A person's accumulated knowledge, the ability to use and accumulate that knowledge
Fluid intelligence	A person's ability to use knowledge and to reason in order to solve novel problems
Quantitative reasoning	A person's ability to engage in quantitative reasoning and to manipulate numerical symbols
Reading and writing ability	A person's basic reading and writing skills
Short-term memory	A person's ability to use information in working memory over a short time span
Long-term storage and retrieval	A person's ability to store and retrieve information during thinking and problem solving
Visual processing	A person's ability to work with visual representations and patterns
Auditory processing	A person's ability to understand and discriminate among auditory stimuli
Processing speed	A person's ability to perform automatic processes, particularly when under pressure
Decision and reaction time speed	A person's reaction or decision times on tasks requiring fast, immediate response

The research data clearly show that when people have a high score on an intelligence test, they are likely to show a similar score if they retake it; similarly, people scoring low on one administration of the test will likely generate a low score on subsequent testing. An individual's scores on different tests of intelligence tend to be similar, too.

Furthermore, scores on these tests tend to be similar over time. The correlation between a child's IQ scores at age 6 and at age 17 or 18 is significant; in one classic study, it was .77. When short-term fluctuations in performance were accounted for, the correlation between IQ scores around age 6 and age 18 was .86; the correlation between scores around age 12 and age 18 was .96. This latter correlation is an exceedingly high value for the measurement of a construct as complex as intelligence.

Reliability is an important characteristic of testing, but more important is the validity of the measurement. If a test measures a stable trait well, the result of the test is valid. It is important to distinguish between reliability and validity. It is possible for a test to be reliable but not useful. That is, a test taker might obtain the same score in repeated testing sessions, but if the test results are not useful in making predictions of certain behavior, the test is not valid for that assessing that behavior.

For example, if a person were tested with a personality inventory for his or her ability to complete a workplace task successfully, that person's score might be stable, that is, reliable, but the test score would not predict job performance very well. In other words, the test would not be valid for that use.

In the workplace, the Myers-Briggs Type Inventory (MBTI) is widely used for making employment decisions. However, many psychologists believe that it is reliable but not valid in predicting success in the workplace. In this instance, a person's score on the MBTI is likely to be stable over time, but not particularly useful for making decisions.

There are two types of validity that are germane to intelligence testing. **Construct-related validity** relates to whether a test actually taps the construct of intelligence. Given that we don't have a complete picture or definition of intelligence yet, it is not entirely clear what intelligence really means. So it is difficult to identify a precise level of construct-related validity of intelligence tests. Nonetheless, many psychologists are satisfied that intelligence tests show decent construct-related validity.

Predictive validity relates to how well intelligence tests act as good predictors of some future behavior. The tests predict academic success reasonably well, which is not surprising given that they are based on activities associated with education. But the pattern is mixed regarding occupational success. The connection between IQ score and job success is fairly low for people in occupations that involve simple tasks. As the nature of the work becomes more complicated, however, intelligence seems to be more important, and the correlation between

IQ score and job success is considerably higher than it is for simple jobs. Furthermore, people with high IQ scores tend to end up in relatively high-status jobs. So intelligence tests show at least a moderate degree of predictive validity for some behaviors.

RECENT THEORETICAL SPECULATION ON INTELLIGENCE

Psychologists have known since the early years of mental measurement research that intelligence is not a single or a simple construct. There are multiple abilities that either reflect intelligence or that may constitute types of intelligence themselves. Recently, there have been attempts to incorporate the diversity of intelligent behavior into models of intelligence.

Howard Gardner's Theory of Multiple Intelligences

Howard Gardner has proposed a widely known theory of multiple intelligences to try and capture the different variety of human capabilities. He initially proposed seven intelligences in his 1983 book, but he has since expanded it to include two others. They appear in Table 4.2.

TABLE 4.2

Types of Intelligences Proposed by Howard Gardner

Proposed Type of Intelligence	Examples of Characteristic of the Type of Intelligence
Spatial	Spatial awareness, ability to visualize spatially, ability to solve puzzles
Linguistic	Ability to communicate verbally, tell stories, remember facts
Logical-mathematical	Mathematical ability, abstract reasoning
Bodily-kinesthetic	Skill in physical and motor activities, ability to build and make things
Musical	Sensitivity to auditory stimuli, including verbal stimuli
Interpersonal	Awareness of others' moods and emotions, ability to empathize
Intrapersonal	Awareness of one's emotions, understanding of the self
Naturalistic	Relating to the natural environment
Existential	Spiritual or religious capacity

Gardner developed his specific intelligences based on several criteria. He suggested that a particular dimension could be considered an intelligence if the abilities associated with it (a) could be diminished through brain damage, (b) had a place in evolutionary history, (c) showed core operations, (d) was amenable to symbolic expression, (e) showed a developmental progression, (f) was expressed through people with exceptional skills, and (g) received support from experimental psychology and psychometric findings.

With these criteria, it is theoretically possible to test Gardner's theory and explore its utility in understanding human intelligence. Unfortunately, there has been little empirical or experimental exploration of Gardner's theory. For this reason, psychometricians have not yet regarded it as a viable theoretical model. In fact, some critics deny its scientific status, saying that its tenets are not falsifiable, an important characteristic of scientific ideas.

Howard Gardner has developed a theory that posits nine different intelligences. (Photo by Kris Connor/Getty)

Furthermore, some critics have suggested that Gardner's concepts may be tautological—that is, an idea may define a second idea, then the second idea is used to define the first. For instance, a person may be proficient in music because he or she has high musical intelligence, and he or she has high musical intelligence because of great musical ability. The reasoning is circular, and there might be no way to test the idea's validity independently. If scientists cannot test the validity of an idea (that is, to see if they can determine that it is false), it is not scientific.

Additional criticism has questioned whether talents should be considered intelligences. The definition of intelligence can be quite vague to begin with, but the issue becomes even more difficult when one tries to differentiate a type of intelligence, which would be a significant characteristic, and a talent, which is a relatively minor ability.

Despite the controversy surrounding Gardner's theory, some educators have embraced his ideas as a useful model for developing educational practices. The different types of intelligence supposedly connect to differences in learning styles across people. For example, according to this model, auditory learners may respond better to spoken textbooks than to traditional, printed text. Or people who are highly kinesthetic may respond better to movies or documentaries presenting material that they can then mimic. Unfortunately for the model, there seems to be little evidence to support enhanced learning as a result of presentation of information based on preferred learning style, as you will see later in the chapter.

At this point, Gardner's model of multiple intelligences is an interesting hypothesis, but research that would support it is lacking. Psychologists recognize the importance of dealing with diverse manifestations of intelligence, but there is currently no empirical evidence to indicate that the model will ultimately be useful in understanding the concept of intelligence and its implications for people's lives.

Robert Sternberg's Triarchic Theory of Intelligence

Robert Sternberg has developed another multifaceted approach to intelligence. Unlike Gardner's model of specific intelligences, Sternberg's model is associated with different processes involved in intelligence rather than with content- or modality-based intelligences.

Sternberg's model proposes that intelligence is reflected in successful functioning in everyday life. One type is **analytical intelligence** that corresponds to traditional measures of intelligence. People who are high in analytical intelligence are successful educationally because they can solve well-defined problems that have a single correct solution, the type of problem that students generally encounter in Western educational systems.

A second type of intelligence in Sternberg's model is **creative intelligence**. People who can solve problems on the spot and who can "think on their feet" to generate novel solutions to problems are said to show high creative intelligence. Some people do not test well on standardized intelligence tests but are remarkably proficient in their areas of expertise. Such people would not have high IQs on traditional intelligence tests even though they are successful in some other area.

A final type of intelligence is **practical intelligence**. This intelligence deals with how well people cope in complex situations of everyday life where any problem has more than one potentially useful solution.

Sternberg's model of intelligence has generated some empirical support. For example, in one study that he and his colleagues conducted, some students with pronounced strengths in one of his proposed types of intelligence (analytical, creative, or practical) were placed in classes with an instructional style that matched their respective strengths. Other students were in mismatched classes. The results were complex and open to different interpretations, but students who completed the class with an instructional style that matched their dominant type of intelligence tended to outperform those in mismatched classes. Sternberg argued that the research supports learning styles, but critics have suggested that the evidence is weak and that, in any case, the instructional strategies did not match those currently promoted by advocates of using variant learning styles in education.

Emotional Intelligence

The awareness that intelligence extends beyond abilities associated with educational endeavors and intellectual factors has led to speculation that perhaps people may differ systematically in their emotional responses to other people and situations. If there are consistent differences across people in their emotional responses, it might be legitimate to regard emotional intelligence (EI) as a type of intelligence that is as real and valid as the intellectual intelligence, practical intelligence, or kinesthetic intelligence that various psychologists have proposed.

Not All Learning Happens in School

You would not expect children who cannot pass an arithmetic test in school to be particularly proficient with numbers. In contrast, children who do well on arithmetic tests are likely to be good with numbers and, as a rule, they will perform well on standard IQ tests.

Psychologist Robert Sternberg has suggested, however, that some children who do not do well on school-based arithmetic tests may be quite adept in everyday use of numbers. He has pointed out that some children in Brazil who earn money by selling goods on the street do quite well in handling money and making change correctly, even though their performance in school is relatively poor.

According to Sternberg, it is critical to be aware of this discrepancy between academic intelligence and practical intelligence. His triarchic theory of analytical, practical, and creative intelligences postulates that there are important differences among various types of intelligence and that by focusing on a single type, which is traditionally the analytical intelligence, we miss important aspects of intelligent behavior. Sternberg has generated data that support his theory, but there are critics who question his approach.

According to psychologists Peter Salovey and John Mayer, people who are high in EI are aware of and can use their emotions in adaptive ways. There have been popularizations of this theory, but Salovey and Mayer have noted that some of these go well beyond what they have characterized as emotional intelligence. Their conceptualization includes four components of EI: managing emotions, understanding emotions, using emotions to facilitate thinking, and perceiving emotions accurately in oneself and in others.

Researchers have found that the reliability of measurement of EI is high. In contrast, validity may be high or low. According to Salovey and Meyer, if EI is associated with a person's ability to attend to and deal with emotions, this ability might be associated with a lower level of psychiatric symptoms. In fact, research has revealed that the higher a person's EI, the lower the reports of problems like headaches and difficulty in concentrating. Furthermore, research has also revealed that males with lower levels of EI show more problems with social adjustment and greater use of alcohol and other drug use.

Emotional intelligence is a fairly new concept, so its definition and the way it is measured are still in flux. And there are critics, including Howard Gardner (who developed the idea of nine different intelligences), who have wondered whether the concept of EI stretches the meaning of intelligence too far. The ultimate scope of the concept of EI remains to be seen, but it is clear that empirical support for the concept exists.

BIOLOGICAL AND ENVIRONMENTAL ASPECTS OF INTELLIGENCE

Psychologists have been trying to find out where intelligence comes from for a long time. One potential source is biological, another is environmental. The prevailing consensus is that you cannot ignore either potential source, a consensus that recognizes that a single answer regarding the source and nature of a construct as complex as intelligence is unlikely.

There is a clear connection between genetics and intelligence, although one's genetic makeup is far from being a perfect predictor of intellectual functioning. In testing this connection, investigators examined patterns of IQs among people who are related and among people who are not related.

Consider the studies of twins. Identical twins result when a single ovum (egg) is fertilized but then splits into two different organisms. These twins are known as monozygotic twins because they originate from a single zygote (a single fertilized egg) and have the same genetic makeup. When members of a twin pair are raised in the same household, the correlation between their IQ scores is strikingly high. But by itself, this finding could indicate either the effect of identical genetic makeup or the effect of growing up in a shared environment. (The results may also reflect some factor that affects twins when they develop in the mother's uterus, which would be a biological effect but not a genetic effect.) The patterns appear in Figure 4.1.

Fig. 4.1 Correlations Among Children with Varying Genetic Similarity and Rearing Condition

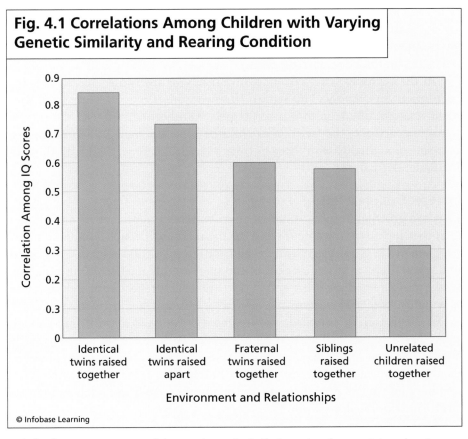

© Infobase Learning

Relation between IQ scores and degree of genetic similarity and environmental overlap. Genes and environment both contribute to IQ scores, but genes may play a larger role for individuals.

If identical twins are raised in different households, the correlation between IQ scores is still high, but it is lower than when they are raised together. These patterns suggest that there is a strong genetic component but that environment does exert some influence.

In contrast to identical twins, there are also fraternal twins. Fraternal twins result when two ova (eggs) are fertilized separately. They are known as dizygotic twins because they arise from two different zygotes, each with its own genetic makeup. Fraternal twins share the same overlap in genetics as any sibling pair. They just happen to be born together. So fraternal twins are no more similar genetically than would be the first and last born brothers and sisters in a family.

In examining the relation between IQs of fraternal twins, we see that there is a high correlation between IQ scores, but not as high as that of identical twins who were either raised together or raised apart. However, even though fraternal twins and any two siblings share the same proportion of genes, fraternal twins are more alike than non-twin siblings. This pattern again suggests that shared environment is important because fraternal twins experience a more similar environment than do non-twin siblings.

As the degree of genetic overlap diminishes for any two people, so does the correlation between their IQ scores. However, the effect of a shared environment remains, although to a lesser degree. Another indication of the importance of genetics is the fact that as children grow up, their IQ scores start to correlate more highly with those of their biological parents than with those of their adoptive parents.

Extreme Environments

Children grow up in many different environments and each environment dictates to some extent the amount and the nature of intellectual stimulation they experience. On the negative end of the continuum, a child might be neglected and ignored by parents or caregivers and there is little intellectual stimulation. As we move toward the other end of the continuum, reflective of a child raised in a highly enriched environment, intellectual stimulation increases.

The effect of an enriched, stimulating environment is positive, although many psychologists believe that high levels of enrichment do not necessarily create children with highly superior intellectual ability. In contrast, however, psychologists generally recognize that children who receive little stimulation and have no control over their environments are usually not likely to demonstrate superior intellectual ability.

Here it is necessary to digress a little to examine the concept of enriched, stimulating environment and how it can backfire. There are, for example, products that claim to enhance the intellectual development of infants (e.g., increases in vocabulary). Among these are DVDs that are sold in a variety of stores and are bought by conscientious parents who want to give their children all the "right" intellectual stimulation available. Unfortunately, researchers Frederick Zimmerman, Dimitri Christakis, and Andrew Meltzoff have found that exposure to DVDs that sold under the claim that they enrich a child's environment (and vocabulary) are actually more closely associated with a decrease in vocabulary among infants.

Other research reveals that the effect that such products have on children varies, depending on interaction with parents after viewing videos. This research suggests that it is the nature of the interaction between parents and children that affects the child's development rather than some artificial stimulus. Psychologists Robert Bradley and Bettye Caldwell have documented several factors that are parent-centered and associated with enhanced intellectual development. These include emotional and verbal responses to children, providing opportunities for exploration and varied stimulation, and avoidance of punishment, all behaviors that can be practiced even in households with limited means. The research supports the idea that parents who are not able to spend large amounts of money on enrichment can produce children who perform as well in school as children raised in households that can afford such products.

Unfortunately, when stimulation is totally lacking, the effect on intellectual development can be negative or even devastating. Psychologists have long seen the effects of neglect in orphanages and foundling homes when workers paid no individual attention to babies. The result is that babies in such environments fail to develop language skills and show an overall listlessness that reflects mental retardation. If this neglect is remedied early enough in the course of the child's development, problems can be eliminated. If not, it stands to reason that the problems can become worse and have long-lasting effects.

So which factor, genetics or environment, determines intelligence? The consensus is that heredity sets a given individual's intelligence level somewhere within a given range. Scientists refer to an individual's lower and upper bounds of intellectual potential as the **reaction range**. When a child develops in a relatively normal environment, the actual manifestation of intelligence will fall at some point within the range, suggesting that both factors have something to do with it.

EXTREMES OF INTELLIGENCE
Intelligence seems to be normally distributed in the population. This means that the majority of people fall around the average and, as you move from the average, there are fewer and fewer people at either end of the continuum. Intelligence tests are typically normed so that the average is 100 and the standard deviation is 15.

The standard deviation is important because it lets us know how far, on average, people are likely to fall from the mean. The majority of people fall within one standard deviation above and below the average. Only about 5 percent are more extreme than 2 standard deviations from the mean. Of this 5 percent, half will score extremely low and half will score extremely high.

Figure 4.3 shows the percentages of people in the population at each IQ level. The lowest range of IQ scores is associated with mental retardation or intellectual disability. The highest range of scores is associated with giftedness. Giftedness is harder to characterize than retardation because giftedness can take many different forms and is less associated with IQ score.

Intellectual and Developmental Disability
The widespread use of intelligence testing arose during the First World War and led to the dubious conclusion that half of the population of the United States was mentally retarded. As psychologists have demonstrated, there were

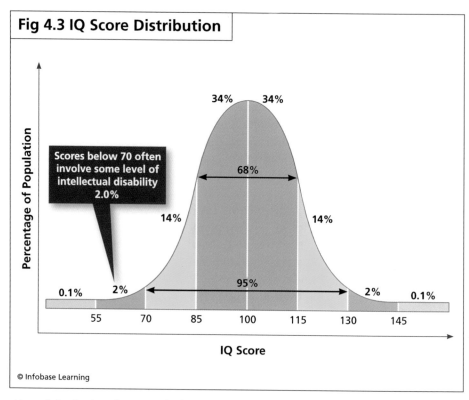

Fig 4.3 IQ Score Distribution

Percentage of Population

Scores below 70 often involve some level of intellectual disability 2.0%

34%   34%

68%

14%   14%

0.1%   2%   95%   2%   0.1%

55   70   85   100   115   130   145

IQ Score

© Infobase Learning

Normal distribution of IQ scores in the population. About 2% of people score in the range associated with intellectual disability. Between 15% and 20% show borderline disabilities (IQ = 70–84). The average score is typically standardized at 100 with the standard deviation of 15.

problems both with the tests themselves and with the conclusions that psychologists drew based on those tests. Scientist Stephen Jay Gould highlighted many of the problems, pointing out that social issues often intruded into the scientific realm. This problem has not yet been solved.

In spite of the difficulties in creating a new subdiscipline within psychology, psychologists began to identify and study people with low IQ scores, classifying those people in different ways depending on their test scores. Table 4.3 shows the categories of what has been termed mental retardation, although as the terminology has evolved, the word *retardation* is now often replaced with the phrase *developmental disability* or *intellectual disability*. In addition, words that were once used as technical terms (such as *idiot, imbecile,* and *moron*) have fallen into disuse, in part because they have assumed derogatory connotations in everyday language. These terms were originally used because they derived from the Greek word for *ignorant person* (idiot), the Latin word for *feeble* (imbecile), and the Greek word for *fool* (moron).

The terminology related to developmental or intellectual disability is still not entirely standard, and the IQ scores associated with the various categories can differ from one group to another. Furthermore, IQ level is no longer the sole criterion used in diagnosis; professionals take everyday functioning into account, so a person with a low IQ score who functions normally on a day-to-day basis would not be diagnosed as retarded. Even with the variability in classification, however, the categories and cutoffs that appear in Table 4.3 are generally descriptive of the way professionals view them.

TABLE 4.3
Current and Historical Terms for Different Types of Developmental Disability (Mental Retardation), the IQ Scores Associated with the Categories, and the Attainable Behaviors of People Within Those Categories

IQ score	Less than 20	20–34	35–49	50–69	70–84
Current term	Profoundly mentally retarded	Severely mentally retarded	Moderate mentally retarded/ Trainable mentally retarded (The term is ill-defined, with different cutoffs specified)	Mildly mentally retarded	Borderline intellectual functioning
Behaviors	Rudimentary speech at most; limited ability for self-care; constant supervision required	Basic self-care skills; able to live in group homes; some communication skill	Trainability, with educational levels usually not exceeding second grade level	Nearly self-sufficient, with educational attainment to roughly the six grade level	Normal, but low, functioning in everyday tasks; ability to hold simple jobs
Historical term	Idiot	Imbecile		Moron	

Are Nations Getting Smarter?

Scientists have argued and debated the relative influence of environment and heredity on intelligence. There is no arguing that intelligence is related to genetic makeup. But over the past several decades, an interesting environmental effect has appeared. Researchers still do not know exactly why this effect has surfaced.

Over the past quarter of a century, James R. Flynn has studied IQ changes in nations since the 1930s. The average IQ scores of a very wide range of countries rose regularly since that time. Figure 4.2 shows the pattern for five countries. In the United States, according to psychologist Ulric Neisser, it appears to have risen in children at an average of 3 IQ points per decade. Psychologists now refer to this pattern of increase as the **Flynn Effect**.

Some researchers have speculated that this increase has begun to level off and may stop, at least in highly industrialized, developed countries. But in underdeveloped nations, it may persist.

It is difficult to ascertain the exact reason for the increases in average IQ score, but highly likely factors include better nutrition and education, greater complexity in the environment, lowered rates of disease and infection, smaller families, and better education with its attendant improvement in children's test-taking skills.

The increase has occurred so rapidly that it can not be attributed to genetic changes. Genetic factors take many generations to have a widespread effect.

(Opposite) **The average IQ of nations around the world has increased over the past five decades. All five countries shown here have experienced significant increases over time The value of 100 for each country reflects a standardized value so that earlier decades can be compared against it. The apparent differences across countries are an artifact of plotting the data this way; those differences are not real.**

Researchers have discovered that the majority of cases of intellectual disabilities arise from unknown causes. The major biological causes of retardation include Down's syndrome, a genetic abnormality of the 23rd chromosome; fetal alcohol syndrome, caused by alcohol consumption by the mother during the development of the fetus; and a genetic abnormality referred to as 22q11.2 deletion syndrome, which involves the absence of a segment on the 22nd chromosome.

Other causes include factors such as infections contracted by the mother during pregnancy, oxygen deprivation during the birthing process, iodine deficiency, and malnutrition. Children who are raised in environments characterized by extreme lack of stimulation and care may also show signs of mental retardation.

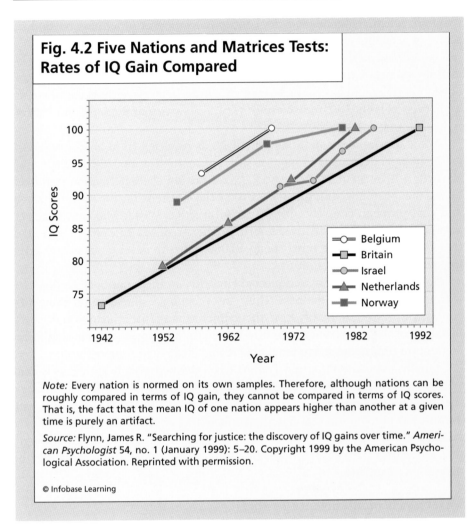

Fig. 4.2 Five Nations and Matrices Tests: Rates of IQ Gain Compared

Legend:
- Belgium
- Britain
- Israel
- Netherlands
- Norway

Note: Every nation is normed on its own samples. Therefore, although nations can be roughly compared in terms of IQ gain, they cannot be compared in terms of IQ scores. That is, the fact that the mean IQ of one nation appears higher than another at a given time is purely an artifact.

Source: Flynn, James R. "Searching for justice: the discovery of IQ gains over time." *American Psychologist* 54, no. 1 (January 1999): 5–20. Copyright 1999 by the American Psychological Association. Reprinted with permission.

© Infobase Learning

Giftedness

Just as some people score low on IQ tests, there is a group that scores extremely high. The initial studies of giftedness by psychologist Lewis Terman focused on academic and intellectual ability. Terman identified a group of academically gifted children in the 1920s and studied them until his death in 1956. Terman's successors continued to study these individuals through adulthood and into old age. At the time Terman initiated his research, many people believed that gifted children would not be successful as adults. Terman showed, however, that the children typically lived successful lives as adults some of those in Terman's studies showed exceptional achievements. Interestingly, his initial screening missed some children who became quite successful. Subsequent to Terman's research, scientists broadened the conceptualization of giftedness beyond IQ scores or academic success.

Giftedness is now associated to a degree with high IQ scores, but psychologists do not regard a person as gifted simply on this basis. For example, psychologist Joseph Renzuli has characterized giftedness in terms of three components: high levels of ability, a strong commitment to a particular domain, and creativity within that domain.

Some psychologists describe giftedness as resulting from an aptitude that exists independent of training. In this conceptualization, giftedness is not learned; it is intrinsic to the person. A contrasting characterization of giftedness is that people become gifted because of the interrelationships among family and environment, coupled with extensive practice. Writer Malcolm Gladwell advanced this latter perspective, describing the so-called "Rule of 10,000 Hours" that posits that a person must spend 10,000 hours to develop ideas and skills that lead to exceptional ability.

Some psychologists have connected Howard Gardner's multiple intelligences with varying types of giftedness. Thus, an exceptional athlete might show giftedness with respect to bodily-kinesthetic intelligence. That athlete would have a high level of ability, a strong commitment to his or her sport that led to significant amounts of time dedicated to practicing it, and creativity in competition.

Finally, psychiatrist Darold Treffert has described what is known as **savant syndrome** in which a person shows some type of remarkable ability even though that person has a notable developmental disability. This condition is rare, and Treffert has pointed out that not all people with a developmental disability are savants, nor are all savants developmentally disabled. It does appear though, that among the rare savants with intellectual disabilities, about half may be diagnosed as autistic.

Social Issues in Intelligence Testing

Since the advent of widespread intelligence testing about a century ago, there have been persistent problems with respect to social and cultural factors and such testing. In early versions of the original test used by the United States Army in the First World War, questions like *Who is Christy Matthewson?* (a famous baseball player of that era) quite obviously reflected a cultural bias. Such questions may have been reasonable for many people, but those unfamiliar with American culture or sport would have been baffled.

There was also a version of the test designed for people who could not read. One component of this test was a picture-completion section in which test takers would fill in missing elements. There were several pictures of people, places, or things that the population for which the test was intended would likely not have recognized, a fact that suggest their answers may not have provided useful test results.

Nonetheless, because scientists have not yet identified exactly what intelligence is, we have to rely on tests with items that we hope reflect intelligence. Common types of test questions include series completion items (e.g., what number comes next in this series: 2, 4, 6, 8, ___), matrix reasoning that involves abstract nonverbal reasoning like spatial reasoning, or judgments of which object in a collection does not belong with the others.

Figure 4.4 shows examples of matrix reasoning (A), identification of the object that does not belong (B), and a historical example of picture completion (C). The first two illustrate question types from the Wechsler Intelligence Scale for Children; the third involves items of the type on the Army Beta tests from the First World War.

The first two types of questions pictured here are generally predictive of how well students perform in school, in part because students often face questions like this in their school work. As such, the exam can be seen as testing what students have already learned rather than some intrinsic characteristic. The third set of pictures that require completion are similarly bound to culture. These images are similar to those used on the Army Beta test, but the question is whether people who could not read or write, many of whom spent their lives on farms in rural areas could be expected to answer them. As you look at these pictures, you may not know what some of the images represent and even if you do know, you may not know what is missing.

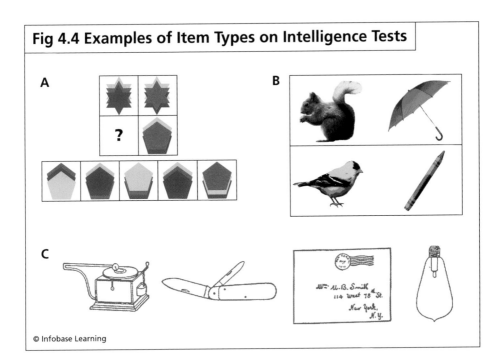

Fig 4.4 Examples of Item Types on Intelligence Tests

A

B

C

© Infobase Learning

The item that completes the matrix in A is image 4; the item that does not belong is the crayon. The items from the Army Beta require a little more discussion.

The first image depicts a phonograph for playing records. You may not know what it is because technology has made phonographs obsolete. People who lived in isolated rural areas in 1917 may never have seen one either. So an inability to identify the object, much less to say what is missing, would not say much about a person's intelligence. The second item is a common pen knife (or jackknife) that most boys of the era would have had. The missing element is the rivet that held the two sides of the knife together. Even if you have a pen knife, it is probably glued together or the rivets, if there are any, are hidden.

The third image is a letter. The missing element is the stamp. Today's students often suggest that a return address or the zip code is missing. But if you consider that this test was designed for people who could not read or write, you will recognize that this image is inappropriate because if you cannot read or write, you don't receive or mail many letters.

The fourth item is a light bulb. It is missing a filament. The problem with this item is that people from rural areas often did not have electricity, so they would not have any use for a light bulb.

Current intelligence tests are more sophisticated than the Army's World War I-era tests and show reasonable validity in predicting academic success. Nonetheless, if a test taker is not familiar with the culture associated with the test, it will not be a very good indicator of intelligence.

CONCLUSION

Intelligence is a concept that we are all familiar with. We generally believe that we can tell the difference between people who are highly intelligent and those who are not. But the process of actually measuring intelligence has always been difficult. Part of the problem stems from the fact that we don't really know what intelligence is, even if we are good at identifying specific behaviors that show high or low levels of intelligence.

For over a century, psychologists have tried to develop measurements that would reliably distinguish between more and less intelligent people. The work has succeeded in some limited respects. Contemporary intelligence tests do a decent, but not perfect, job of predicting academic performance and, to a lesser degree, career success.

Everybody knows that people can show high levels of performance in one domain but be average or below average in another. The dominant model that has emerged is that people have a fundamental level of intelligence, often referred to as g for general intelligence, that is correlated with many other, more specific aspects of intelligence. Recently, psychologists have expanded the definitions of intelligence in ways very different from those of earlier psychologists;

research is still needed to assess how useful the broader definitions will be in describing and predicting people's behaviors.

Finally, we cannot ignore the fact that there have been many social issues associated with intelligence testing. There is no single test that is not influenced by social and cultural factors. It is not clear that psychologists will ever be able to create so-called culture fair tests.

Further Reading

Deary, Ian J., Alexander Weiss, and G. David Batty. "Intelligence, Personality, and Health Outcomes: How Researchers in Differential Psychology and Chronic Disease Epidemiology Are Collaborating to Understand and Address Health Inequalities." *Psychological Science in the Public Interest* 11, no. 2 (August 2010): 53–79.

Gottfredson, Linda. "The General Intelligence Factor." *Scientific American Presents* 9, no. 4 (1998): 24–29. http://www.udel.edu/educ/gottfredson/reprints/1998generalintellige ncefactor.pdf. Retrieved April 10, 2011.

Gould, Stephen J. *The Mismeasure of Man.* New York: W. W. Norton, 1981.

Neisser, Ulric, Gwyneth Boodoo, Thomas J. Bouchard Jr., A. Wade Boykin, Nathan Brody, Stephen J. Ceci, Diane F. Halpern, et al. "Intelligence: Knowns and Unknowns." *American Psychologist* 51, no. 2 (Feb 1996): 77–101.

Pashler, Harold, Mark McDaniel, Doug Rohrer, and Robert Bjork. "Learning Styles: Concepts and Evidence." *Psychological Science in the Public Interest* 9, no. 2 (Dec 2008): 105–119.

CHAPTER 5

LEARNING: CLASSICAL AND OPERANT CONDITIONING

Behavior is complicated and hard to predict. But some psychologists believe that the rules governing behavior are very simple. According to behaviorists, you act the way you do because you have been rewarded for doing so, and you refrain from doing other things because you have been punished for doing them.

Naturally, applying these simple rules is not easy, but in spite of their simplicity, these rules have been surprisingly fruitful in helping psychologists gain insights into patterns of behavior. Much of the research that scientific psychologists have conducted has involved animals, often rats or pigeons, but the results of their studies have applicability to people, too.

Throughout the history of psychology, there has long been a debate about the specific causes of human behavior. This debate has played out in a variety of ways. For example, the debate over whether behavior is driven largely from internal causes (such as described by Sigmund Freud) or external causes (as described by Skinner) has long fueled controversy and discussion in the field. In this chapter, we will discuss the perspective that the causes of behavior emerge as a result of the interaction between the environment and organisms.

Different points of view gained and lost popularity for much of recorded history as people attempted to understand human behavior. Those theories, though, like much of the work on human behavior, arose from speculation based on logic. In the past 150 years, since the work of Charles Darwin, scientists have taken seriously the idea that science should test claims about behavior empirically. Psychology began as an attempt by Wilhelm Wundt and his contemporaries to understand how we sense and perceive the world around us, and how we think. Somewhat later, other psychologists changed the focus of psychology toward observable behaviors. In this chapter we will explore the main theories and the people who helped shape the behavioral approach.

In our discussion, you will see that understanding human and animal behavior relies on the knowledge that our environment controls our behavior. In this chapter, the term *learning* will refer to the way that we acquire knowledge about the world through interactions with our environment. *Acquiring knowledge* will mean how our behavior changes and is shaped by our environment. References to **behaviorism** will allude to a philosophy of human behavior as described by B.F. Skinner (and, to a lesser degree, by John B. Watson). There will also be references to an area known as **applied behavior analysis**. This is an area that takes the field of learning and applies it to socially relevant problems. The goal of practitioners in this area is to use basic, theoretical research principles to develop more applied research that extends our knowledge to a setting in which we are able to use what we know to improve some situation or problem.

CLASSICAL CONDITIONING

The typical description of learning starts with a discussion of classical conditioning, the area of learning developed and made famous by the Russian physiologist Ivan Pavlov. Pavlov's research established some fundamental principles regarding how environmental contingencies shape behavior; that is, he showed that certain conditions in the environment could lead to predictable behaviors.

However, discussions of learning or behaviorism did not start with the work of Pavlov. There were philosophers, such as John Locke, who believed that external forces control behavior. It was Pavlov, though, who provided empirical evidence to demonstrate that change in behavior is a result of an environmental change.

Pavlov's research on behavior was actually serendipitous; that is, he was investigating digestion of food, not learned behavior. In fact, he won the Nobel prize in 1904 for his work on the physiology of digestion. While engaged in his research on digestion, he noticed a surprising and unpredicted aspect of learning that became known as classical conditioning. He was measuring salivation, the first component of digestion, as a result of exposure to meat powder. He noticed, though, that the dogs in his experiment began salivating when in the presence of the people who provided the food, even before the food appeared. If salivation was part of digesting food, he wondered, why would the animals begin to salivate even when there was no food present?

This observation and the question that resulted spurred Pavlov to study the conditions under which salivation would occur in the presence of an initially neutral stimulus. Pavlov noticed that if he paired the food with a neutral stimulus, such as a tone, enough times, the tone would eventually elicit the salivation, even without the food. After many replications and variations of conditions Pavlov concluded that the animal learned to associate the tone with the food and, thus, salivated. Pavlov conducted research over many years, documenting the conditions in which reflexive behavior like salivating would occur and how it might be eliminated. He even developed a rudimentary model of how classical conditioning could lead to mental illness.

Many people are familiar with the terminology of classical conditioning. In Pavlov's research, the food (the meat powder) served as the **unconditioned stimulus** (the stimulus that naturally leads to a response), the salivation as the **unconditioned response** (the naturally occurring response), the tone as the **conditioned stimulus** (the learned stimulus), and finally, salivation in response to the tone as the **conditioned response** (the learned response). According to Pavlov and American psychologist John B. Watson, this is how humans learn their patterns of behavior. Based on their ideas, considerable excitement arose over the fact that we could change what gave rise to a reflexive response.

Watson is often credited with being the person who really popularized behaviorism and the study of learning. In 1913, Watson wrote a paper that described his dissatisfaction with the work that many psychologists were carrying out. The paper, called "Psychology as the Behaviorist Views It," forged a new direction based on the idea that psychology should be treated as a natural science with all the trappings of a science. To that end, Watson emphasized empiricism (observation) and careful measurement. In his view, psychology could be a discipline like physics in which theories were developed, tested, and either found to be true or eventually discredited. He believed that to develop a carefully designed psychology, we needed to focus on what we can observe (behavior) not speculate about what we cannot observe (thought).

To demonstrate this important shift in theory, Watson carried out a series of observations and experiments in which he attempted to demonstrate that classical conditioning can give rise to emotional responses, such as fear. Emotional responses are, in fact, reflexive responses. If we can train a dog to salivate through classical conditioning, perhaps we can use the same principles to explain how people learn to be afraid of things in their lives.

In a well-known study, Watson and his graduate student (and later his wife) Rosalie Rayner attempted to condition a young child (little "Albert," aged 1) to demonstrate a fear response in the presence of a white rat. This study appears in just about every discussion of John Watson's career. Interestingly, though, historians of psychology generally believe that Watson and Rayner were not really successful in their classical conditioning endeavors. Moreover, reports that the subject's fear of the white rat generalized to other white, furry things have not withstood scrutiny. So the story about Albert seems to be an anecdote that illustrates the principles of classical conditioning rather than an example of true classical conditioning.

Nonetheless, as noted above, Watson wanted to examine the behavior, and not to infer what was going on inside the head of the child. Fear, an internal and unobservable response, was to be demonstrated through behavior, such as crying or moving away from an object that Albert did not initially fear and, in fact, found to be an interesting plaything.

The experiment worked like this: Albert was brought into the lab and was presented with the rat. When the rat was placed in front of him, he tried to play with it, was interested in what the rat was doing, and was demonstrating behavior that would seem to indicate that he was positively oriented toward the animal. During the conditioning phase, Watson put the rat next to Albert at the same time another person struck a metal bar behind the child's head. The sound made by the metal bar surprised Albert, and he showed a fear response (e. g., crying, trying to move away from the rat, whimpering). After six presentations of the rat and the noise simultaneously, Albert showed fear of the rat alone. In addition, Watson claimed that the fear generalized to include other white or fuzzy things such as a Santa mask, a fur coat, and a rabbit.

The principles of classical conditioning are relatively easy to identify here and are outlined in Figure 5.1. The principles can be generalized beyond this example and relate to the conditioning of just about any emotional or reflexive behavior.

As noted above, historians of psychology have concluded that Watson's conclusions were overstated. Nonetheless, Watson was convinced that all human behavior is acquired in such a manner. In fact, according to Watson's earlier 1913 paper, all we really need to do to control human behavior is to control the human environment.

Psychologists have learned how to develop a behavior. But we also know that behaviors can be unlearned. In research on learning, eliminating a behavior involves a process called **extinction**. If we apply this to the case of Watson and Rayner's study with Albert and the white rat, for example, continuously presenting the rat without the sound would eventually extinguish the fear and we would no longer see the fear response to the rat. Sometimes, however, the fear to the conditioned stimulus (in this case the rat) will spontaneously reappear, although the response will not be as strong as it was when the initial conditioning took place; this phenomenon is known as **spontaneous recovery**.

Classical conditioning has been implicated in the emergence of phobias. The idea is that there is an incidental association between a previously neutral stimulus and a fear-inducing stimulus that leads to a response. The neutral stimulus then causes the fear response. So, for example, you might be afraid of heights because you once fell. The fall led to the fear, but the incidental height (which

Fig. 5.1 Principles of Classical Conditioning

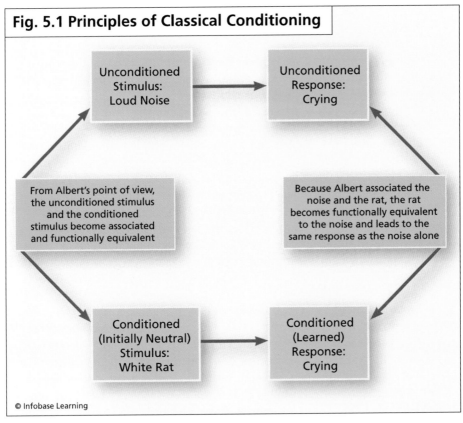

Principles of classical conditioning as Watson and Rayner would apply them to the case of Little Albert.

is neutral) might be associated with the fear-inducing stimuli, and you might then develop the phobia. To treat such issues, psychologists often try to break the association through a variety of simple, behavioral procedures through a process called **systematic desensitization**. The principles are simple, but applying them is somewhat more complicated.

This process involves identifying the object or the situation associated with the phobia. Suppose somebody is phobic about snakes, so much so that even a picture of a snake elicits extreme fear. A therapist might work with someone to find ways to diminish the such overwhelming fear, suggesting, for example, that the person might think of a snake that is very small, very far away, and not moving. Even though there might be some fear associated with thinking about the snake at all, the person is likely to try this and might be able to do it. After repeated focus on this image of a small, distant, and immobile snake, the person may begin feeling somewhat comfortable with that image. As time goes on, that

Classical Conditioning and Food Avoidance

Sometimes people have a very specific dislike for a food, such that the prospect of eating it makes them feel sick. In some instances, the reason for this response can be related to classical conditioning.

Consider what would happen if you ate something and then got sick. Although that food might not have had anything to do with your getting sick (you might have been coming down with something), when the opportunity to eat that food came up again, you would probably avoid that food as the thought of eating it would make you nauseous.

This phenomenon is known as **taste aversion**. Your body somehow is able to remember what you ate just before getting sick, and your body makes the connection between the food and the illness. It is as if nature had prepared us to be able to learn automatically when a particular food is not good for us.

This phenomenon was first reported by psychologist John Garcia who observed changes in the behavior of rats when they became ill after exposure to radiation that he administered in his research. They seemed to associate the illness with the water they were drinking because they began avoiding the water.

In people, this kind of association is rather common. One example of how taste aversion can occur can be seen with people undergoing chemotherapy treatment for cancer. They associate the food they eat with the discomfort caused by the therapy when, in reality, the food is not relevant to their discomfort. A more light-hearted example of this involves psychologist Elizabeth Loftus and actor Alan Alda. Loftus managed to implant a false memory in Alda, specifically that he had gotten sick after eating deviled eggs. After the memory was implanted, the actor seemed to avoid hard-boiled eggs, illustrating how easily we may be predisposed to conditioned taste aversion.

Garcia's research was striking because it revealed that conditioning occurred after a single trial. In most instances, classical conditioning requires multiple trials. Another remarkable aspect of conditioned taste aversion is that people experience it without conscious awareness.

comfort level continues to grow and the fear response to that specific image of snakes will be extinguished.

The therapist might then ask the person to imagine that snake moving its head just a little. This may induce some discomfort, but the initial success may encourage the person to take this next step and it is likely that the person will eventually think about the image if a snake with a moving head without extreme fear. After a while, that image will become less fear provoking.

With such systematic, small steps, the therapist may ultimately help the person feel more comfortable thinking about a snake being nearby, holding a picture of a snake, being in the presence of a snake, and ultimately, maybe even holding a snake. What will have taken place is a systematic process whereby the person becomes desensitized to the anxiety associated with the snake.

Therapists need to be well trained to use such a technique because dealing with phobias is always going to be more complicated than the simplified description given here. Still, what is clear is that if a phobia arose as a classically conditioned response, it is possible to develop a program that extinguishes the phobic response behavior.

OPERANT CONDITIONING

In 1920, John Watson was involved in a scandal that led to a divorce from his wife, Mary Ickes (who had been a student of his at the University of Chicago) and subsequent marriage to Rosalie Rayner (then a student of his at Johns Hopkins University). Because of the scandal, he was forced to leave his position at Johns Hopkins University; he entered the business world and became very well known in the world of marketing and advertising.

Even with the departure of the leading proponent of behaviorism, this approach came to dominate psychology. However, the focus shifted from understanding behavior by examining the antecedents of behavior (what came before it) to examining the consequences of behavior (what happened after this behavior). One of the most influential psychologists of this movement was B.F. Skinner. In fact, it is probably correct to say that Skinner was the most influential psychologist during the period spanning the 1940s to the 1960s.

Skinner argued that although Watson's ideas were important, psychologists needed to address questions of the types of behaviors about which classical conditioning was silent. He argued that classical conditioning explains some aspects of behavior involving automatic or reflexive behavior quite well. However, he also argued that we need to examine the consequences of behavior rather than the precursors of behavior. Specifically, we need to examine how the consequences of behavior serve to shape our behavior in the future. Thus, whereas Pavlov and Watson studied responses that were elicited by some stimulus, Skinner studied what causes organisms to initiate behaviors and how the results of those behaviors influence future action.

According to Skinner, there are two categories of consequences that follow behavior: reinforcement and punishment. **Reinforcement** serves to increase the probability that a behavior will occur again, and **punishment** serves to decrease the probability that a behavior will occur again.

Skinner also posited that there are different ways to administer both reinforcement and punishment. When something is given to an individual to serve as a reinforcer, it is called **positive reinforcement**. In everyday use, we often refer to positive reinforcement as reward. And as we all know, a reward will increase the likelihood that a behavior will recur.

There is another way to increase the chance that a particular behavior will occur. When people (or animals) are experiencing something negative, they work to make it stop. If the negative condition is removed, they are likely to

Whatever Happened to Little Albert?

Since John Watson's famous study with Little Albert and the white rat, people have wondered "Whatever happened to Little Albert?" For psychologists, the overarching question has been "Whatever happened to the classically conditioned phobia?" Did Albert continue to fear white things for the rest of his life? Or did he develop the ability to deal with this fear—either on his own or through some form of alternative conditioning? The uncertainty and speculation have persisted for nearly 100 years, mostly because Watson never provided any follow up to what happened to his most famous study participant.

A number of articles attempting to answer both questions have recently been published. In 2010, two psychologists claimed to have discovered the identity and fate of Little Albert. In their article, they report that Little Albert was really Douglas Merritte, the child of a nurse named Arvilla Merritte, who worked at Johns Hopkins Hospital. According to this article, Arvilla received $1 for allowing young Douglas to participate in Watson's study. The authors were able to piece this together using historical documents and birth records. The article goes on to say that Douglas, unfortunately, died at the age of 6 due to hydrocephalus. Thus, they concluded, it was impossible to know for sure if any conditioning ever generalized across situations or if the child had developed fear that could not be overcome.

The mystery took another turn when an issue of *American Psychologist* included articles by various authors who argued that Douglas Merritte could not have been Little Albert. The authors of these articles suggest that descriptions of Douglas Merritte did not match the available descriptions of Little Albert closely enough, and that the difference were significant enough to preclude a conclusion that the two children were the same child. Claiming that the identity and fate of the child Albert is still in question, these authors posited that an answer to the burning question of "Whatever happened to the classically conditioned phobia?" could still be answered.

Psychological historian Ben Harris has pointed out that the stories created about Little Albert over the decades constitute *origin myths* that psychologists of different eras have generated as psychology has evolved. Nonetheless, the number of studies devoted both to the original research and to the identity of Little Albert attest to the importance that psychologists of these different eras have attached to John Watson's work.

repeat their successful behavior the next time it occurs. This situation describes **negative reinforcement**.

Both types of reinforcement lead to an increased probability that a behavior will recur. With positive reinforcement, the behavior leads to getting something desirable; with negative reinforcement, the behavior leads to removing something undesirable.

There are parallel conditions regarding punishment. When people engage in some behavior and are punished for it, they are less likely to perform that action in the future. When a punisher is actively applied, it is called a **positive punishment**. (Note that the word *positive* here does not mean good. In this case, as in the case of positive reinforcement, it means to apply.)

In contrast, when something desirable is removed after people engage in some behavior, they are less likely to act that way in the future. This situation describes **negative punishment**.

In both reinforcement and punishment, *positive* means that something is applied (e.g., a reward like a smile or a punishment like a being yelled at), whereas *negative* means that something is taken away (e.g., being in "time out" ends when a child apologizes or the child does not get dessert if it does not eat vegetables at dinner). This concept is often misunderstood because the terms *positive* and *negative* are unfortunate in that they carry with them the idea of good and bad. The easiest way to understand the distinction is that reinforcement always *increases* a behavior, and punishment always *decreases* a behavior. In the case of reinforcement and punishment, it is more useful to think of positive as giving and negative as removing. Positive and negative reinforcement and punishment are easier to understand with examples, as shown in Table 5.1. Note especially that negative reinforcement actually increases the probability that a behavior will occur again.

Skinner also argued that we how we administer reinforcement and punishment impacts the effectiveness of the consequence. He claimed that one goal of psychology should be to predict and control human behavior. In order to do so, we need to completely understand the influence of reinforcement and punishment on behavior. Punishment, according to Skinner, is something that ought to be used either very rarely or not at all. If punishment is used, Skinner recommended that it be immediate, consistent, and severe enough to actually be punishing. If it is not, it will not effectively control behavior.

Skinner also claimed that punishment has some undesirable consequences. For example, spanking is a common form of punishment by parents. According to some research, the aggressive nature of punishment is often imitated by the person receiving the punishment. That is, if a child is spanked for doing something that the parent does not approve of, that child may imitate the same aggressive behavior when encountering something he or she finds displeasing or annoying.

TABLE 5.1

Examples of Positive and Negative Aspects of Reinforcement and Punishment

	Something is applied: Positive	Something is taken away: Negative
Increases Behavior	**Positive reinforcement** • Praise for good behavior • Money for chores • Bonus for sales	**Negative reinforcement** • Put on seatbelt to turn off a buzzer in the car • Buy child candy to get the child to stop crying (This is negative reinforcement for the parent and positive reinforcement for the child.) • Take away chores for good behavior
Decreases Behavior	**Positive punishment** • Corporal punishment • Soap in mouth for swearing • Extra chores	**Negative punishment** • Time out • Take away cell phone • Take away privileges

Suppose, for example, a child is spanked for writing on the wall. The punishment is designed to decrease the probability of the child writing on the wall again. However, the child might then "spank" his little brother for playing with his toys, with the intent of decreasing the chances that little brother will play with them in the future. This is probably not the outcome parents desired and and one reason Skinner argued that punishment should be used sparingly.

A second problem with punishment is that it indicates what behavior to avoid but does not give any information about what behavior might be appropriate or desirable. Punishment, from Skinner's perspective, could be more effective if it included (or was directly followed by) clarification of desirable alternate behaviors.

A third drawback about the effectiveness of punishment in changing behavior in the long run is that the person being punished may refrain from engaging in the undesirable behavior only when the person doing the punishing is around. If the person administering the punishment is not around, the person engaging in the undesirable behavior recognizes that it is safe to keep doing so because punishment happens only when the punisher witnesses the behavior.

Skinner argued that in the long run, reinforcement is more effective than punishment because reinforcement gives a clear signal about what behavior is appropriate and provides a desirable outcome for person (or animal) engaging in such behavior. In his research, Skinner documented that there are efficient ways to set up a structure for administering reinforcers. He emphasized that reinforcement need not be administered every time desirable behavior occurs, and researchers have demonstrated that long-term change in behavior is actually more likely to come about if intermittent reinforcement is applied once a behavior is established.

The reasons for this are many, but the simplest way to understand this concept is through an example. Suppose a person decides that she is going to train her dog to come in when called. As part of the training, she gives the dog a treat every time it comes when called. If the dog receives a treat each time, and if there is never a time the dog returns and is not reinforced, the behavior is likely to drop off dramatically if it does not receive a treat. The dog might come in a few times with no treats but might not come in after that. Alternatively, if the dog only gets treats sometimes, and it's not easy to predict when the treats are coming, the dog will continue to behave as desired even in the absence of treats for a longer period of time.

Psychologists refer to this as schedules of reinforcement. Table 5.2 presents examples of the schedules and how they work.

TABLE 5.2
Examples of Schedules of Reinforcement

	Interval Schedules	Ratio Schedules
Fixed Schedules	**Fixed Interval:** reinforce after a certain fixed amount of time has gone by. • Pay check every 2 weeks • Favorite show on the same time every day.	**Fixed Ratio:** reinforce after a certain fixed number of behaviors have occurred. • Get paid for every 10 lawn mowers sold • Receive money for every 5 As on a report card
Variable Schedules	**Variable Interval:** reinforce after time has gone by, but the amount of time between reinforcers varies. • Checking for email that may come after random periods of time • Visiting a restaurant that a famous athlete patronizes on occasion	**Variable Ratio:** reinforce after a number of behaviors have occurred, but the number of behaviors required for reinforcement varies • Winning at a slot machine in a casino • Finding returnable soda bottles behind a store on occasion • Finding a desired music CD in a used music store every now and then

So far, we have been discussing established behaviors. But what happens in cases where desirable behavior has not yet occurred? In other words, if something hasn't happened, how can it be reinforced? Consider, for example, that much behavioral research has involved rats pressing levers or pigeons pecking at stimuli in laboratory apparatus. Because rats don't naturally press levers and pigeons don't naturally peck at lab apparatus, psychologists had to begin their behavioral research by devising ways to get the animals to engage in those behaviors.

Skinner became adept at building behaviors in the laboratory. He would initially reinforce any behavior that was remotely close to the desired behavior. When that behavior was repeated, he would not reinforce it again but would wait until the animal emitted a behavior that was closer to the desired behavior. Little by little, Skinner would demand more of the animal until it performed the way Skinner wanted. This process is called **shaping**.

It is useful during shaping to provide a lot of reinforcement immediately and then taper off to an intermittent schedule so that the behavior will persist even in the absence of frequent reinforcement. People can also be vicariously shaped with this pattern of reinforcement by watching others. Psychologist Albert Bandura showed in several studies that both reinforcement and punishment influence an observer's subsequent behavior, a process called **social learning**.

B.F. SKINNER AND BEHAVIORAL TECHNOLOGY

B.F. Skinner believed that the principles of behaviorism were applicable to many different facets of life and was firmly committed to a behavioral technology that would lead to the betterment of society. But this was a controversial belief that frightened or angered as many people as it inspired. At other times, his ideas were simply dismissed as impracticable.

During World War II, for example, Skinner became interested in conditioning pigeons in a way to help the war effort. Pigeons are very visually oriented animals, so Skinner proposed training pigeons in the laboratory to learn to peck at pictures of bombing targets. Once they had mastered this, they could be harnessed into a bomb-dropping apparatus and sent aloft. When they saw the real target, they would peck at a guidance system the way they had been conditioned to do in the laboratory, thus guiding the bomb to the target. Although Skinner was confident that the procedure would be effective, the military was not interested. The lack of interest in his proposal frustrated Skinner because, based on what scientists knew of behavioral theory, the system could well have been successful.

Skinner also devised a machine that would help students learn. It involved what was called **programmed learning**. The learning occurred in small steps so that the student would receive positive reinforcement for virtually every response, and each response built on the previous one. In the end, the student would have a grasp of the entire body of material to be learned. Educators used this approach for a short period during the 1950s and 1960s, but it fell out of favor by the end of the 1960s when behavioral approaches to psychology and education were replaced by more cognitive approaches.

The most controversial of Skinner's inventions was his air crib, which was a sophisticated, climate-controlled playpen that would allow a child to play unencumbered by layers of clothing and would filter the air to reduce the incidence of exposure to germs. The air crib was designed with behavioral principles in mind.

Skinner used the air crib with his daughter Debra when she was an infant. Some people derisively referred to the design as "baby in a box," and rumors circulated that Debra later became psychotic and attempted suicide. These rumors were entirely false (Skinner's daughter turned into a healthy and productive adult), but people who thought that Skinner's learning theory dehumanized people were often willing to accept them.

Many people resisted Skinner's ideas because they thought that he viewed (and even defined) people as organisms entirely lacking in free will and completely controlled by the environment, something his detractors strongly objected to. Toward the end of his career, Skinner wrote *Beyond Freedom and Dignity*, a book in which he discussed what he saw as the problems associated with the belief in free will in humans. He maintained that this belief keeps us from structuring our environment in ways that are conducive to reinforcing productive and pro-social behavior.

APPLICATIONS OF LEARNING

Learning theory has been hailed by many as the key to understanding human behavior. And, in fact, learning theory does explain a great deal about human behavior. If we assume these two points as true, then we must also assume that to understand human behavior, we really need to understand the context in which behavior occurs. Human behavior does not occur in a vacuum. In fact, the context of human behavior is extraordinarily important in understanding why humans do the things that they do.

One application of learning principles that has been very helpful can be seen in the classroom. We have found that much of human behavior in the learning environment can be improved by controlling the environment in which that behavior occurs. So teachers can improve the learning of their students by controlling the environment in which the learning takes place, specifically in the classroom where learning is to occur. Consider how this works if a teacher is interested in helping students in his class develop good social behavior. The teacher begins by developing a reward system for some appropriate behavior. For example, each time a student raises his or her hand instead of just calling out, a checkmark is chalked next to the student's name on the blackboard or

Applied Behavior Analysis and Autism

The incidence of diagnoses of autism spectrum disorder has increased dramatically over the past decade. The research on autism has been wide and varied and there has been a great deal of controversy over what causes autism and how we can treat this debilitating disorder. Regardless of the cause(s), the symptoms include impaired social functioning, low levels of effective communication, and, in many cases, behavior disorders that make it very difficult for a child with autism to integrate into a traditional social setting.

Psychologists have used learning theory in the form of applied behavior analysis (ABA) to treat the disorder, and over the last 25 years, practitioners of ABA have developed a variety of techniques to deal with its symptoms. For example, one of the hallmarks of autism is that autistic children cannot follow very simple directions. A typically developing child will, with a small amount of prompting, develop the ability to respond appropriately to a parent's request for a particular behavior. A child with autism will not.

An ABA therapist can work with a child with autism and provide a highly structured setting to assist the child in learning and even mastering to some extent appropriate responses to simple requests. This might begin with some as basic as teaching an autistic child to respond to his or her own name. This is accomplished by applying the principles of behavior and reinforcement theory: In a highly structured environment the child receives reinforcement for performing a desired behavior. The therapist uses the reinforcement steadily to shape the behavior so that it occurs with a high level of frequency. After the behavior is well established, the reinforcement is withdrawn and provided only intermittently. The use of procedures like ABA has given many children with autism the ability to integrate more effectively into society.

on a paper list designed to record such behavior. For every 5 marks, the student earns some simple but desirable reward. Through such a process, the teacher is able to establish desirable behavior by controlling the environment and the reinforcement associated with behavior in that environment.

Interestingly, researchers have discovered that reinforcement can sometimes be detrimental to behavior. When people receive rewards for behaviors that they enjoy, they may begin to alter their thinking about those behaviors. That is, the student's motivation for doing something changes from internal (i.e., enjoyment) to external (i.e., the reward). The students observe their own behavior and conclude that the reason they are engaging in it is really the reward, not the enjoyment. And if the reinforcement stops, the behavior may be extinguished. This fact makes it clear that implementation of behavioral theory needs to be well researched and well planned before it is applied by people without a strong background in psychology.

One widely accepted application of learning theory is in the area of autism treatment. Psychologists trained in and practicing applied behavior analysis have found that it is a very effective strategy for helping individuals make adjustments that allow them to function better in society. One way to do this is to help autistic children improve their linguistic skills. Here again (as in the classroom example above) one important prerequisite is to establish some control over environment. In this case, to understand how to develop linguistic skills in an autistic child, a therapist can first create a detailed description of the child's environment and then work on modifying that environment in ways that promote developing basic linguistic skills. This happens as the therapist provides small units of reinforcement for general approximations of the desired behavior.

CONCLUSION

In general, behaviorism or learning forms the basis of much of what we know about psychology. The basic principles of behaviorism and learning relate to different aspects of human behavior and how the environment contributes to the control and prediction of behavior. Many aspects of human and animal behavior can be understood by examining the conditions under which a given behavior occurs. That is, when we know that an individual's behavior is reinforced by something specific and we learn to use positive reinforcers that reward that behavior (or conversely, negative reinforcers to punish that behavior) judiciously, we can control that behavior by promoting it or discouraging it.

Further Reading

Beck, Hall P., Sharman Levinson, and Gary Irons. "Finding Little Albert: A Journey to John B. Watson's Infant Laboratory." *American Psychologist* 64, no. 7 (Oct 2009): 605–614.

Harris, Ben. "Letting Go of Little Albert: Disciplinary Memory, History, and the Uses of Myth." *Journal of the History of the Behavioral Sciences* 47 (2011): 1–17.

Skinner, Burrhus Frederic. *Beyond Freedom and Dignity*. New York: Knopf/Random House, 1971.

CHAPTER 6

THE BIOLOGY OF THINKING

HOW THE BRAIN IS INVOLVED IN LEARNING

Learning takes place as a collection of individual neurons becomes active, causing a different set of neurons to respond until many neurons and several different parts of your brain are involved in a single memory. Most of the time, learning seems effortless and automatic. Most of the time, in fact, you aren't even aware that you are learning. And yet learning happens even during the most mundane daily routines. The reason you are not aware of it is that it is mostly a "behind-the-scenes" process, so you don't experience any great rush of activity in your brain while it is happening.

What you learn can also be rather mundane and often seems more like memory than learning. You can, for example, remember where you left your coat when you entered your house, where the car is parked, or what you talked about with your best friend. And chances are, you probably had no idea you were learning something as you remembered these things, but you were. This might be easier to understand if you recall that the models of memory that psychologists have developed provide good descriptions of the kinds of learning that take place. These include such things as declarative and procedural memory; or sensory, short-term, and long-term memory. But these models of memory are really only descriptions of the outer manifestations of learning. The actual learning involves changes in the way that your brain responds to certain stimuli.

In fact, every time you learn something, your brain is permanently changed. Scientific psychologists have documented that individual neurons change structurally in the process of learning. So after reading this paragraph, you are physically different than you were before you read it. The amazing part of learning is that, even though your brain constantly changes as a result of it, there seems to be no limit to the amount of learning that a person can achieve. Or, to put it more simply, your brain will never be full.

Researchers have used sophisticated technology that has emerged in recent years to document some of the physiological processes involved in learning. We now have the ability to focus in on increasingly smaller areas of the brain as learning and thinking take place, so that it is possible, using computerized technologies, to determine with significant accuracy whether a person is thinking of a tool or an animal. We still cannot "read" a person's mind, but we can identify which parts of a person's brain are activated when he or she is thinking about different concepts.

Researchers have also studied people who have experienced brain damage in order to see how their capabilities have changed as a result of the brain damage. Studying people with brain injuries was initially the only way that scientists could investigate the role of various parts of the brain in thought, so the first speculations about learning and the brain were quite general. Then psychologists began studying the behavior of animals whose brains were experimentally altered, and this paved the way to begin thinking about human brains and behavior. Now we can gain very specific information about neuronal activity in the brain and how it connects to thought. Scientists can even temporarily shut down some parts of the brain to see what happens when some particular area is deactivated.

Over the past few decades, psychologists have developed an increasingly sophisticated view of the processes associated with learning and thinking, starting with how individual neurons in the brain function when we learn and working toward understanding how the varied parts of the brain are associated with learning a single thing. As much as we have learned, though, some important questions remain unanswered.

THE BRAIN AND MEMORY

There is a widespread myth that people use only 10 percent of their brain. If this were true and people actually did not use the other 90 percent, neither serious accidents nor diseases that destroy brain tissue would matter much—we would all be able to function just fine with the parts of the brain still working. Unfortunately, destruction of even a small amount of brain tissue can have devastating consequences because everything you do requires the active use of many parts of your brain, even for tasks as simple as recognizing an object placed in front of you, learning a list of words, or assembling a jigsaw puzzle.

Consider what takes place in your brain when someone places a hammer in front of you. You can see what the object is, where it is, and what color it is; you can also think about how someone would use a hammer. If you've ever held a hammer in your hand, you will know how it feels in your hand even if you don't pick this particular hammer up. You may also have a fleeting thought about the last time you used a hammer to fix something or hang a picture, etc. Obviously there is a great deal of cognitive processing taking place here. Not so obvious is the fact that this seemingly simple scenario, each part of which seems simple and automatic, involves many parts of the brain and much additional activity in the body as your brain responds.

You might first move your eyes to be able to see the hammer, an activity which is controlled by a structure in your midbrain called the superior colliculus. In addition, shifting your attention to the hammer would involve your prefrontal cortex, and paying attention to the hammer would include activation of cells in your parietal lobe. In addition, identifying a tool would involve yet other brain areas, your premotor gyrus and your middle temporal gyrus in the left hemisphere of your brain. There is also evidence that your left hemisphere is involved in encoding information (like what tools you have seen), whereas your right hemisphere is involved in retrieval of information (like remembering hanging that picture). Recognizing where the hammer is and how you would use it cause activation of two different areas outside of the primary visual cortex. Furthermore, different cells in the brain might become active if you start thinking about using a hammer. If you subsequently try to remember who was involved in presenting the hammer, it again requires activity in the prefrontal cortex.

All of this processing happens spontaneously and immediately when you glance at a hammer placed in front of you. You are not aware of the way your brain integrates different types of information, but damage to brain tissue can interrupt normal information processing and reveal that even simple thoughts require many different parts of the brain. The sidebar on seeing shows how complicated vision really is and how big a role the brain plays in the way vision works.

The Hippocampus and Declarative Memory

One particular brain structure that is involved with memory is the **hippocampus**. The hippocampus has received a lot of attention for its role in declarative memory. Research has revealed that people and experimental animals with lesions in the hippocampus are unable to form such memories. Undoubtedly, the most famous person associated with hippocampal damage is known in the research literature as **H.M.**

As a child, H.M. suffered brain damage as a result of a bicycle accident. This brain damage led to extreme, uncontrollable seizures that plagued him in

Seeing Without Seeing

Asking a blind person to engage in a visual task does not seem to be a very smart thing to do. But researchers have discovered that, in some cases, blind people can actually see. One of the strange aspects of the situation is that, even though a person may deny being able to see anything, he or she may be able to behave like a sighted person in certain ways.

Neuroscientist Lawrence Weiskrantz studied a person identified as DF who suffered brain damage because of lack of oxygen and was subsequently unable to name objects or describe any characteristics of those objects. In addition, she denied being able to see the objects.

During one session, Weiskrantz asked her to indicate the size of a block by using her thumb and index finger to show its size; her estimations were entirely wrong, reflecting that she had no awareness of the actual size of the block. Nonetheless, she was able to reach out and pick up the block, holding her thumb and index finger the appropriate distance apart to do so.

Similarly, she could not describe how she would hold a postcard in order to insert it into a slot (like a mailbox). Still, she could put the card in the slot if asked to do so.

Weiskrantz labeled this phenomenon **blindsight**. More recently, other scientists have reported similar phenomena, with people showing appropriate responses to auditory stimuli, tactile stimuli, and smell stimuli. In each case, people show an inability to process information in one way but can respond automatically another way.

The reason that people might be able to behave appropriately without conscious awareness of the stimuli to which they are responding is that awareness requires that neurons send information to the appropriate parts of the brain for identification and for language. These neural pathways are not the same ones that are responsible for knowing where an object is or how to orient toward it.

Scientists have speculated that humans (and other animals) have evolved parallel systems for processing visual information. One system may mediate quick responses to stimuli, whereas the other involves slower thought processes. In the case of blindsight, if a person suffers damage to the pathways associated with identification and language, but the pathways involved in processing location or movement are still intact, useful information about the object is still being processed. So the person is able to see without being aware of seeing.

adulthood. In an attempt to stop the seizures, he underwent bilateral removal of the hippocampus, the paraphippocampal gyrus (which we now know is important in memory), and the amygdala (also relevant to memory). The result was permanent anterograde amnesia; he could not form any new declarative memories. He also experienced some retrograde amnesia involving memories for the three years prior to the surgery. His seizures abated for about a year, but unfortunately, both major and minor seizures returned thereafter. He died in 2008 at age 82, 55 years after surgery that destroyed his ability to form declarative memories. At his death, his identity as Henry Gustav Molaison was revealed.

Prior to research on H.M., scientists had no idea that the hippocampus was so pivotal in the memory process. Over the decades, however, the hippocampus has been seen as a key structure in learning. One phenomenon associated with the hippocampus is the change in the structure and functioning of neurons that takes place during learning. This change, called **long-term potentiation (LTP)**, involves greater sensitivity of neurons to stimuli. When learning has taken place, the axon terminals increase in a neuron, and the dendrites in the receiving neuron become more sensitive. You can see how such a change could be associated with learning, which is an enhanced response to what you have learned.

Psychologists generally believe that memories are not stored in the hippocampus itself. Rather, the hippocampus seems to facilitate transfer of information from short- to long-term memory in the association cortex. When tissue in this cortex is damaged, specific memories may disappear, whereas destruction of hippocampal tissue does not affect specific memories.

The role of the hippocampus is quite complex. It appears that the hippocampus in the right hemisphere processes memory for spatial information while the left hemisphere processes verbal information. In addition, different parts of the hippocampus are active in encoding and retrieval of information.

Even with all the knowledge that scientists have gained, there is still uncertainty about the types of memory associated with the hippocampus. When H.M. underwent removal of his hippocampus, his declarative memory system was obliterated, but he was still able to acquire procedural knowledge. This finding led psychologists to speculate that the hippocampus is involved only in declarative memory.

Experimental research with animals has also supported the idea that the hippocampus is associated with declarative memories. A rat placed in a radial arm maze can learn which arm in the maze holds food. A researcher can set up a study so that the animal either has to remember which arm held the food or so that the animal learns to associate an illuminated bulb with the presence of the food.

With this experimental setup, investigators assumed that learning to identify the appropriate arm of the maze involved declarative memory, whereas learning to move to the light was more akin to procedural memory. When the researchers destroyed tissue in the hippocampus, the rats were no longer able to identify which arm of the maze had food, but they performed normally at moving toward the light to find food.

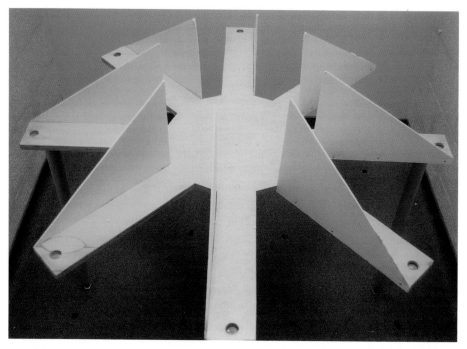

A radial arm maze used in memory research. Animals that have had tissue in the hippocampus destroyed have a hard time learning which arm of the maze has food, but they can learn to move toward an illuminated light bulb that signals food. *(Wikipedia)*

On the other hand, when a different part of the brain (the caudate nucleus in the forebrain) was lesioned, the animals were able to use declarative memory (they remembered food was in one arm of the maze and not the other), but their performance on the procedural task was impaired (they didn't remember that moving toward the light would bring them to the food).

Memory damage of the type experienced by H.M. is fairly rare, but a similar problem does arise on occasion in heavy alcohol users. When an individual engages in heavy drinking, the result can be a vitamin B1 (thiamine) deficiency. This problem can lead to hippocampal damage and severe memory loss. The hippocampal damage seems to be responsible for the anterograde amnesia that these people experience. They also suffer from retrograde amnesia, although the cause of this memory loss is still uncertain. The problem is known as **Korsakoff's syndrome**.

The Basal Galglia and Procedural Memory

Most research on memory throughout psychology's history has focused on declarative memory. This type of memory, sometimes subdivided into semantic and episodic memory, has a lot to do with who we are. Semantic and episodic memory relates to what we know and the personal experiences about our lives that we remember. H.M. spent 55 years without forming any new declarative memories. In his own mind, he was always 27 years old and could not even recognize his own image as an older adult.

The Limbic System and Thought

The hippocampus is located in the forebrain, particularly in the **limbic system**. The limbic system mediates emotional arousal and emotional responses. It may seem a little strange at first to consider emotional structures of the brain in a discussion of learning and thinking. However, emotion can play a central role regarding what we remember.

Specifically, the **amygdala** is implicated in memory for emotional events. When a person acquires declarative information, the amygdala is useful in pairing that declarative memory with the accompanying emotion.

This pairing is seen as the basis for vivid flashbulb memories. A commonly used example involves the terrorist attack on the World Trade Center in 2001. People generally say that they know exactly what they were doing when they first heard (or saw) the tragedy. Such vividness may result from the pairing of the hippocampal and amygdalar responses.

You should remember, though, that even though people have very lucid flashbulb memories, the accuracy of those memories is questionable. Research on such memories indicates that they are as prone to error as any other memory.

Some psychologists have suggested that repressed memories may result from a failure of the brain to coordinate the responses of the hippocampus and the amygdala. In stressful situations, the body releases substances (e.g., cortisol) that at lower levels may enhance hippocampal firing but at high levels may inhibit such activity. If the hippocampus does not respond appropriately, a declarative memory may not be formed. The concept of repression is controversial, however; psychologists disagree regarding the extent to which it occurs and under what circumstances.

The role of the amygdala in learning is not in dispute in a general sense. Research has revealed that the amygdala is responsible, in part, for classically conditioned fear. If a drug that inactivates the amygdala is injected into a rat's brain, learning is impaired; conversely, drugs that activate the amygdala are associated with enhanced learning. These findings have implications for treatment of posttraumatic stress disorder (PTSD), which involves unwanted memories for stressful events. If drugs that block formation of memories are given to a person who has just undergone a traumatic experience, the subsequent emergence of PTSD may also be blocked.

However, procedural memory is important in our lives, too, even if it does not relate as closely to our personal identities as declarative memory does. Procedural memory, as noted in Chapter 1, is our memory for the way we do things; it is associated with movement or patterns of behavior.

If you are proficient at riding a bicycle or typing on a keyboard, your procedural memory will be well established. Initially, you have to pay attention to maintaining your balance on the bicycle or finding keys on the keyboard. But after a while, the process becomes automatic, and you are not really aware of the individual motions needed for the behavior.

One area of the brain relating to procedural memory is the basal ganglia. (As you have probably figured out by now, it is generally not appropriate to talk about *the* area of the brain associated with any behavior because there are always multiple areas that come into play.) As described above, rats in a radial arm maze whose caudate nucleus in the basal ganglia were destroyed had trouble with procedural learning.

You may ask whether all of these studies of rats really relate to the way people remember. In fact, the brains of different types of mammals are quite similar in many respects, so what it true for one type of mammal may be true for another. If we can demonstrate that, in rats, the caudate nucleus is important for procedural knowledge, it is worth investigating to see if it is also true for humans.

Case studies of people with Huntington's disease and with Parkinson's disease support the idea that the animal model represents what happens in people. These two diseases involve problems with movement and muscular coordination. Such people have difficulty developing tasks that involve procedural knowledge, but their declarative memories remain unaffected.

It is not surprising that the basal ganglia would be involved in movement. The neurons in the basal ganglia have close interconnections with neurons in the primary motor cortex. The basal ganglia also interconnect with the frontal lobe that helps us plan and control behavior. As a result, scientists have investigated whether there is a connection between the basal ganglia and attention-deficit hyperactivity disorder (ADHD). The research has indicated that people diagnosed with ADHD have a smaller caudate nucleus in the basal ganglia and have problems with connections between the basal ganglia and the frontal lobe. The basal ganglia are also implicated in obsessive-compulsive disorder. It seems fairly certain that the basal ganglia are critical in movement, including procedural memory. In addition, the cerebellum appears to be involved in procedural knowledge.

Hormones, Hunger, and Learning

Researchers have recently identified that a hormone named **ghrelin**, which is produced in the stomach and in the brain, is involved in learning. Ghrelin is the

Not Knowing What You Know

Neuroscientist Larry Squire trained a group of people with anterograde amnesia to solve a puzzle called the Tower of Hanoi. In this puzzle, there are three posts on which you can move stacks of rings, as shown in the illustration. The point of the game is to move all of the rings to another post so that they are in order of size, with the biggest rings on the bottom. There are three rules:

> *You can move only one ring at a time.*
> *You can move only the top ring.*
> *A ring can sit only on top of a larger ring.*

This puzzle takes some time to solve, but with practice, people become very adept at it.

When Squire worked with the patients with amnesia, they improved on the task, reflecting increasing levels of procedural knowledge. Surprisingly, however, when they stopped working on the puzzle and returned to it later, they had no memory of ever having worked on it. Being able to solve the puzzle reveals that they had procedural memory, even if they didn't have declarative memory.

This type of phenomenon reflects the separation between the processes of declarative and procedural memory. In people with amnesia, they literally might not know what they know.

Tower of Hanoi puzzle. People with anterograde amnesia could solve it after practicing on it, even though they had no recollection that they had ever worked on it. *(Shutterstock)*

first circulating hormone associated with hunger. As it wends its way through the bloodstream, it stimulates neurons in the hypothalamus. When a person is hungry, ghrelin levels rise; when a person has eaten, ghrelin levels diminish.

In addition to its role in stimulating hunger, ghrelin also seems to play a role in learning. Investigators have provided evidence for receptors for this hormone in the hippocampus and the amygdala, both of which are instrumental in learning. Various experiments have shown that increased levels of ghrelin lead to enhanced memory, particularly spatial memory. So learning seems to take place because of your stomach as well as your brain.

DEFICITS IN THOUGHT

Researchers have gained significant knowledge about information processing from people who have suffered brain damage. These studies sometimes lead to ambiguous conclusions, however, mostly about the role of particular brain structures because brain damage can be extensive and may involve multiple parts of the brain. The specificity of research conducted with H.M. is fairly rare and was possible because the removal of his brain tissue was highly controlled during surgery. Thus, his doctors and Brenda Milner, the psychologist who worked with him for decades, knew precisely which areas of the brain were destroyed.

The deficits described in this section of the chapter provide glimpses into the brain structures associated with various mental processes and what happens when those structures are damaged. Researchers caution that in some cases, it is not clear whether the effect of damage to a brain structure means that the structure is itself involved in a behavior or whether it is just a pathway through which information flows. In any case, these deficits show that specific areas of the brain control mental functions that normally work together seamlessly; when something goes wrong, it becomes apparent that supposedly unitary mental tasks are not really as simple as they seem and require multiple different brain components.

Episodic Memory

A young Canadian man, K.C., was in a single-vehicle motorcycle accident that led to significant hippocampal damage. After K.C. recovered from the trauma of the accident, his semantic memory was fairly typical. But he had lost his **episodic memory**. That is, although he could perform normally on a test of knowledge and retained memories of his life, he was no longer able to associate any of those memories with his own life experience.

K.C. also suffered from anterograde amnesia and thus lived in the present, just as H.M. did. Unlike H.M., though, K.C.'s memories about his own life were simply recalled as facts without any personal or emotional involvement, somewhat like the memories we have about the lives of other people—facts devoid of personal attachment. A further indication of his cognitive deficit was that he could not envision himself in the future. If asked to tell what his life would be like in a day or a week, he was unable to respond.

The example of K.C. illustrates that different parts of our brains are associated with semantic versus episodic memory. But definitive conclusions can be tricky. Consider, for instance, that K.C. was working on a farm when he was 16 at which point a bale of hay fell on his head, rendering him unconscious. For a period of time after he was released from the hospital, he needed anticonvulsant medication. So it was hypothetically possible that the initial head injury was a contributing factor in the later cognitive deficits he experienced. Hypothetical constructs aside, new technologies (like fMRI) made it possible for scientists to identify areas in K.C.'s brain that were damaged following his motorcycle accident, and the findings confirm the conclusions that other researchers have drawn in related studies.

Awareness of One's Body

When brain tissue in one parietal lobe is destroyed, people often have weakness or paralysis on the other side of the body. The typical pattern is damage to the right hemisphere means subsequent problems with the left side of the body. When this happens, the result may be **unilateral neglect syndrome**, a condition in which an individual becomes entirely unaware that he or she has a left side.

Such people will not wash the left side of their body and may not notice food on the left side of a plate. They can learn that there is something wrong and adjust their behaviors to improve their functioning, but they still lack a fundamental awareness that they have a left side. In some cases, they may see their own left hand or left arm and not recognize that it is theirs. They will claim that it belongs to somebody else. No amount of explanation will convince them that it is theirs because the awareness that they have a left side is gone.

Another, similar problem is **anosognosia**, a condition that arises from damage either to the frontal or parietal lobe. This deficit involves a failure to recognize that there is any impairment; in some cases, people may deny having even major deficits like blindness. The problem is not associated with sensory loss. Nor is it the case that the people are lying; they believe with certainty that they are fully intact. The problem arises because of damage to the parts of the brain that integrate sensory experience and bodily awareness. The anosognosia can be selective: A person may recognize that he or she has multiple bodily impairments while denying that another impairment exists.

Interestingly, when such people are asked about their ability to move a paralyzed left arm, they may believe that they are moving it or have moved it. In the somewhat unusual situation in which they are aware that there is some problem moving the arm, they engage in **confabulation**—that is, they make up a plausible sounding story about their inability to move the arm (e.g., it is the left arm, so it is weaker than the right arm). In some cases, when pressed on the issue, they might temporarily admit to a deficit but will revert to denial soon after this. According to philosopher William Hirstein, anosognosia is a relatively common condition. This assertion was based on a study of paralyzed patients: More than one-fourth of those in the sample group denied any problem.

Awareness of Other People in One's Life

Normally, we recognize people who are important in our lives. In certain cases, however, people cannot. They may see a parent or a spouse and conclude that person is an imposter. This deficit is called **Capgras syndrome** or **delusion**.

Researchers speculate that this syndrome arises when someone recognizes another person as being familiar but does not feel the emotion that people typically experience when seeing others who are important in their lives. Thus, the person afflicted with Capgras draws the conclusion that the look-alike is an impostor. Scientists think that such a response is prompted by a failure of coordination between the temporal cortex, where faces are usually recognized, and the limbic system, which is involved in emotions. Some neuroscientists (including Vilayanur S. Ramachandran, who has conducted extensive research on this delusion) have suggested that there may also be problems with the prefrontal cortex or other areas involved in reality monitoring. This delusion is sometimes also seen in people diagnosed with schizophrenia or with dementia.

Personality and the Brain

Everybody has a unique personality. Although you may be similar to others in some ways, you show traits in ways that are special to you. But in important ways, your personality is simply a function of the way your brain processes information.

The implication of this fact is that if part of your brain is destroyed, your personality may be permanently altered. Perhaps the most famous case of personality being altered by brain damage is that of Phineas Gage, who was injured when an explosive charge he was setting accidentally went off, driving a metal rod into his brain and destroying tissue in his prefrontal cortex. Surprisingly, Gage recovered, but his life significantly changed after the event. Subsequent reports on these changes are not entirely consistent. Some reports note that his behavior was quite aberrant, whereas others indicate that he was able to lead a generally normal life. Some researchers have proposed that descriptions of the extreme changes in behavior were exaggerated and may not have been permanent.

From what we can gather, Gage's personality did change. Once calm and capable and even congenial, he became less sociable and very impatient with others. If one or both of his prefrontal lobes were damaged, it would not be

Phineas P. Gage. *(Wikipedia)*

surprising that negative behaviors emerged because this part of the brain is associated with inhibiting unacceptable behaviors. Other research associates the frontal cortex with personality, and findings from such studies suggest that people diagnosed with borderline personality disorder show lower activation of part of the frontal cortex associated with control over one's emotions. This area, the anterior cingulate cortex, also has connections with the amygdala.

The availability of technology that can map the activation of various parts of the brain as people process different kinds of information is promoting a better understanding of how various parts of the brain work together to create personality. Who you are involves the firing of networks of neurons; when some of those neurons stop working, your personality can change.

CONCLUSION

Our ability to think, talk, learn, and remember generally seems to be easy and automatic with respect to the tasks in which we engage every day. Most of us, however, are not aware of the incredible amount of brain activity that takes place when we complete even the most simple of these tasks.

But any description of the cortical processes associated with thinking is going to be incomplete. We still do not know all of the interconnections among different areas of the brain and how those areas communicate and provide feedback to one another. Nonetheless, psychological scientists have discovered some of the fundamental issues associated with thinking.

One thing that has enabled studies and related findings on this matter is the availability of sophisticated, computer-based technology, which has allowed us to learn about the brain's functioning in normal circumstances as well as when there has been brain damaged. It is safe to say, however, that much more remains to be discovered.

Further Reading

Hirstein, William. *Brain Fiction: Self-deception and the Riddle of Confabulation*. Cambridge, Mass: MIT Press, 2005.

Rosenbaum, R. Shayna, Stefan Köhler, Daniel L. Schacter, Morris Moscovitch, Robyn Westmacott, Sandra E. Black, Fuqiang Gao, and Endel Tulving. "The Case of K.C.: Contributions of a Memory-impaired Person to Memory Theory." *Neuropsychologia* 43 (2005): 989–1021.

Sacks, O. *The Man Who Mistook His Wife for a Hat and Other Clinical Tales*. New York: Touchstone Books, 1998.

GLOSSARY

Alex the Parrot   A grey African parrot that learned speech in a long-term research project aimed at determining whether a parrot can learn language.

algorithm   A series of steps in problem solving that is guaranteed to lead to a successful solution to a problem.

amygdala   Part of the limbic system of the brain involved in emotion.

analytical intelligence   In Robert Sternberg's theory, the type of intelligence that corresponds to traditional, academically related measures of intelligence.

anosognosia   A lack of awareness that prevents people from recognizing that they have impairments such as blindness or paralysis.

applied behavior analysis   An applied area of psychology associated with B.F. Skinner that makes use of behavioral principles in treating people.

arbitrariness   One of the linguistic universals, relating to the fact that words do not have inherent meaning and take on a given meaning only because people use them in a given way; arbitrariness explains why the same concept is represented with different words in different languages.

availability heuristic   A decision-making strategy in which a person makes a judgment about the probability that an event will occur based on information easily accessible from memory about a related event.

base rates   The frequency of occurrence of an event; people often ignore base rates in estimating the likelihood of the occurrence of a related event.

behaviorism   A school of psychology that focused on observable behaviors rather than mental processes; it is often associated with B.F. Skinner and John Watson.

blindsight   The ability to process visual information without conscious awareness that one has that ability.

bounded rationality   A model of decision making that posits that people make decisions based on logic, with the limitation that they do not always have all the information they need, the ability to process the information they have, or unlimited time to consider their decision(s).

Capgras delusion   A belief that familiar people (e.g., family members, a spouse) are impostors because the normal emotion associated with seeing such people has been disconnected from the brain's recognition function.

conditioned response (CR)   In classical conditioning, a response elicited by the conditioned stimulus and closely resembling the naturally occurring unconditioned response.

conditioned stimulus (CS)   In classical conditioning, an initially neutral stimulus which, after learning occurs, leads to the same response as the naturally occurring unconditioned stimulus.

confabulation   Filling in the gaps in one's memory with plausible, but fictitious, details; sometimes occurs as a result of brain damage.

confirmation bias   The tendency to seek out information or to test solutions that support one's beliefs and to ignore conflicting information.

conjunction fallacy   A judgment error in which people believe that in an event space, a member of a subset is more likely to occur than a member of the larger set of which the subset is a part.

connectionist networks   Model of memory which posits that learning involves interconnected networks of information rather than single nodes of memory.

construct-related validity   A term relating to whether a measurement actually assesses the construct or idea that it is supposed to measure.

context-dependent memory   Phenomenon in which one's recall of information is better when recall takes place in the same environment in which it was learned.

creative intelligence   In Robert Sternberg's theory, the type of intelligence associated with being able to apply knowledge in novel and useful ways in everyday situations.

creativity   The production of something that is original and valuable.

declarative memory   Memory for facts and knowledge that one can bring to short-term or working memory.

deductive reasoning A logical process that uses general information to arrive at a specific conclusion; it can be used to prove that something is true, unlike inductive reasoning, which leads to conclusions of what is likely.

displacement One of the linguistic universals, relating to the fact that language is used to refer to events, objects, and so forth that are not physically present.

divided attention Concentrating on more than one stimulus at a time, an ability that most people do not possess with respect to complex cognitive tasks.

encoding The process of transforming incoming stimuli into a form that can be incorporated into the memory system.

encoding specificity A principle stating that retrieval of a particular memory is enhanced if retrieval occurs in the same context as learning or that there is an interaction between characteristics of retrieval information and characteristics of what was learned.

episodic memory The type of memory associated with personal events in one's life.

extinction The process of eliminating a conditioned response or a conditioned behavior by presenting a conditioned stimulus without the unconditioned stimulus (in classical conditioning) or failing to reinforce a behavior that had previously been shaped (in operant conditioning).

fixation In problem solving, focusing on one aspect of a problem and ignoring others that would be more helpful in arriving at a solution.

Flynn effect A term referring to an increase in measured scores on intelligence tests, a phenomenon that has become evident over the years in most countries around the world.

focused attention Concentrating on a single stimulus and ignoring other stimuli.

framing The way an issue is posed or worded, which affects how a person responds to that issue.

functional fixedness A type of fixation in which a person fails to see alternate or unusual uses for an object that can be used to solve a problem.

gambler's fallacy The erroneous belief that a person will have a change of luck after having a run of bad luck because the law of averages will make up for past events.

g-factor In Charles Spearman's theory of intelligence, the single fundamental (or general) element of intelligence that subsumed specific subfactors.

ghrelin A hormone produced in the stomach and in the brain that interacts with the hypothalamus and the hippocampus and enhances learning.

H.M.   The initials of a person with hippocampal damage who was unable to form declarative memories after surgery to reduce seizures. After his death, his identity as Henry Gustav Molaison was revealed.

heuristic   A rule of thumb that a person uses to expedite the decision-making process; it does not guarantee a successful solution but may be generally useful in reaching a decision.

hippocampus   Part of the limbic system of the brain; involved in emotion and memory.

hypothetical construct   An abstract concept that helps psychologists understand or explain a person's behavior, thoughts, attitudes, and so forth.

ill-structured problems   Problems that do not necessarily have an identifiable optimal solution or an obvious path to a successful solution.

incidental emotions   Emotions that are not relevant to a decision being made but that influence the decision anyway.

incubation   The process of arriving at the solution to a problem through mental activity that a person does not experience consciously but that ultimately leads to awareness of a solution.

inductive reasoning   A logical process that draws on past experience or knowledge to help a person make a decision about an uncertain future event.

intelligence   A hypothetical construct originally relating to one's ability to engage in successful problem solving, adapt to the environment, reason, and so forth; its meaning has been expanded to include many different dimensions of human behavior.

Kanzi   A bonobo chimpanzee that psychologists Sue Savage-Rumbaugh and Duane Rumbaugh trained to communicate using a message board to determine whether a chimpanzee can learn language.

learning styles   A hypothesis that posits that different people learn more effectively and efficiently with an instructional style that matches their learning style (e.g., visual, auditory, tactile); there is no solid evidence to support this hypothesis.

limbic system   A set of structures in the brain that are involved in emotion, motivation, and learning.

linguistic universals   Characteristics of language that are said to occur in every naturally occurring language.

long-term memory   Term given to one's permanent, apparently limitless memory capacity.

long-term potentiation   A long-term change in the structure and function of neurons that occurs during learning; in the process, the neuron becomes more sensitive to certain stimuli.

mental set   A type of fixation in which a person attempts strategies based on experiences that may not be helpful in solving a current problem.

mental test   A term coined by James McKeen Cattell to include varied measurements of sensory, perceptual, and cognitive abilities.

method of loci   Mnemonic strategy in which one learns a list of items by mentally placing them along a path during learning and retracing that path and picking them up in retrieval.

misinformation effect   The phenomenon in which providing false information after a person experiences an event can lead that person to incorporate that false information into memory as if it were part of the original memory.

mnemonic devices   Strategies that enhance memory and retrieval.

morpheme   In language, the smallest element that has meaning (e.g. *cat* is one morpheme, and the plural *s* is one morpheme; the word *cats* has two morphemes).

multitasking   Trying to accomplish more than one task at a time, an ability that most people do not possess with respect to complex cognitive tasks.

negative punishment   A type of punishment in which a positive stimulus is removed following a behavior, leading to a decrease in the frequency or probability of that behavior.

negative reinforcement   A type of reinforcement in which a negative situation is eliminated following a behavior, leading to an increase in the frequency or probability of that behavior.

negative transfer   The hindrance in learning or problem solving that results from applying previously learned information to a new situation when applying the old information conflicts with successful resolution of the problem.

Nim Chimpsky   A chimpanzee that psychologist Herb Terrace trained to communicate using sign language to determine whether a chimpanzee can learn language.

overconfidence effect   The phenomenon in which the confidence that people have in their judgments exceeds the accuracy of those judgments, with greater disparity between confidence levels and accuracy levels increasing as the confidence levels rise.

pegword method   Mnemonic strategy in which one learns a list of items by pairing each item to be learned with an item on a previously memorized list and creating a vivid image of the two items interacting with one another.

phoneme   In language, a fundamental sound within a given language.

positive punishment   A type of punishment in which a negative outcome follows a behavior, leading to a decrease in the frequency or probability of that behavior.

positive reinforcement   A type of reinforcement in which a desirable outcome follows a behavior, leading to an increase in the frequency or probability of that behavior.

positive transfer   The benefit gained in learning or problem solving that results from being able to apply previously learned information to a new situation.

practical intelligence   In Robert Sternberg's theory, the type of intelligence associated with how well people cope in complex situations and solve problems that have multiple potential solutions.

predictive validity   The term relating to the degree to which a score or a variable predicts some criterion variable.

proactive interference   A cause of forgetting; specifically refers to the fact that the first of two items to be learned interferes with recall of the second item to be learned.

procedural memory   Memory for how to do something.

programmed learning   A system of learning developed by B.F. Skinner for use in schools; programmed learning relies on reinforcement for correct answers so that students will persist in learning because of the positive reinforcement they receive.

psychometric approach   An approach to measuring intelligence that relies on statistical relationships among various measures of intelligence.

punishment   A consequence that leads to the decrease in the frequency or probability of a behavior.

reaction range   In theories of intelligence, the lower and upper bounds of intelligence generally determined by heredity; the actual level of intelligence would depend on the nature of the environment.

reconstructive memory   The unconscious, automatic process of integrating different memory fragments to conjure up a complete memory; the process can result in erroneous recollection.

recovered memory controversy   Controversy centering around the contention that people can repress traumatic memories for years or decades and then recall them.

reinforcement   A consequence that leads to the increase in the frequency or probability of a behavior.

representativeness heuristic   A decision-making strategy in which a person makes a judgment about an event or an object based on how much that event or object looks like (or is representative of) the typical situation.

retrieval   The process of bringing stored information into working memory.

retrieval failure   A cause of forgetting arising from an inability to "locate" information that one has stored in memory.

retroactive interference   A cause of forgetting that occurs when the second of two items to be learned interferes with recall of the first item learned.

satisficing   In problem solving, selecting the first outcome that is acceptable, even if it is not an optimal choice.

savant syndrome   The presence of some remarkable skill in a person with a notable developmental disability. Not all savants are developmentally disabled, nor are all developmentally disabled people savants.

s-factor   In Charles Spearman's theory of intelligence, subfactors of intelligence that deal with specific behaviors.

shaping   The step-by-step building of a behavior by initially reinforcing behaviors that are only close to the desired behavior, then requiring ever closer approximations to the final behavior.

short-term memory   Term given to information currently in working memory, generally limited to between five and nine chunks of information.

social learning   The application of behavioral principles in understanding how learning takes place even if one does not receive reinforcement but only sees others reinforced for a given behavior.

spontaneous recovery   The reappearance of a behavior that had been extinguished.

state-dependent memory   Phenomenon in which one's recall of information is better if recall takes place while one is in the same physical state during recall as one was in during learning.

storage   The retention of information either in short-term, working memory or long-term memory.

subjective expected utility   A model of decision making that posits that people make decisions by computing the expected value of competing outcomes, then selecting the choice with greatest expected payoff.

synesthesia   The rare condition in which a person experiences a stimulus, like a sound, in multiple modalities, such as hearing the sound while simultaneously experiencing visual and tactile sensations.

syntax   In language, the word order and structure of sentences.

systematic desensitization   A form of therapy for phobias in which a person with a phobia is gradually exposed to anxiety-producing objects related to the phobia so that the phobic response is extinguished over time; the end goal is for the person to face the object that initially generated the phobic response without manifesting fear or anxiety.

taste aversion   An automatic reluctance to eat a food that was once followed by illness, even if the illness was not actually related to the food.

tip-of-the-tongue phenomenon   Phenomenon in which a person who tries to recall a word can retrieve various characteristics of that word (like number of syllables, what sound it begins with, and so forth) but cannot recall the word itself.

unconditioned response (UR)   In classical conditioning, the response that occurs to an unconditioned stimulus without any learning on the part of the organism.

unconditioned stimulus (US)   In classical conditioning, the stimulus that elicits a response without any learning on the part of an organism.

unilateral neglect syndrome   A condition sometimes occurring as a result of brain damage to the nondominant hemisphere in which a person has no awareness of one side of the body, usually the left side.

unnecessary constraints   In problem solving, a hindrance that blocks or slows down arrival at a successful resolution because of self-imposed limiting rules that do not exist in the actual structure of the problem.

vocal-auditory channel   One of the so-called linguistic universals relating to the fact that most languages use sound to communicate. Languages among people who are deaf do not share this feature, even though they are naturally occurring languages.

Washoe   A chimpanzee that psychologists Beatrix and Allen Gardner trained to communicate using sign language to determine whether a chimpanzee can learn language.

well-structured problems   Problems that have a single best solution and a predictable path to that solution.

BIBLIOGRAPHY

Beck, Hall P., Sharman Levinson, and Gary Irons. "Finding Little Albert: A Journey to John B. Watson's Infant Laboratory." *American Psychologist* 64, no. 7 (Oct 2009): 605–614.

Cytowic, Richard E. *The Man Who Tasted Shapes. A Bizarre Medical Mystery Offers Revolutionary Insights into Emotions, Reasoning, and Consciousness.* New York: Putnam, 1993.

Deary, Ian J., Alexander Weiss, and G. David Batty. "Intelligence, Personality, and Health Outcomes: How Researchers in Differential Psychology and Chronic Disease Epidemiology Are Collaborating to Understand and Address Health Inequalities." *Psychological Science in the Public Interest* 11, no. 2 (August 2010): 53–79.

Foer, Joshua. *Moonwalking with Einstein: The Art and Science of Remembering Everything.* New York: Penguin, 2011.

Gottfredson, Linda. "The General Intelligence Factor." *Scientific American Presents* 9, no. 4 (1998): 24–29. http://www.udel.edu/educ/gottfredson/reprints/1998generalintelligencefactor.pdf. Retrieved April 10, 2011.

Gould, Stephen J. *The Mismeasure of Man.* New York: W. W. Norton, 1981.

Groce, Nora Ellen. *Everyone Here Spoke Sign Language.* Cambridge, Mass.: Harvard University Press, 1985.

Harris, Ben. "Letting Go of Little Albert: Disciplinary Memory, History, and the Uses of Myth." *Journal of the History of the Behavioral Sciences* 47 (2011): 1–17.

Hirstein, William. *Brain Fiction: Self-deception and the Riddle of Confabulation.* Cambridge, Mass: MIT Press, 2005.

Loftus, Elizabeth F. "Planting Misinformation in the Human Mind: A 30-year Investigation of the Malleability of Memory." *Learning & Memory* 12, no. 4 (Jul 2005): 361–366.

Luria, A. R., and Lynn Solotaroff. *The Mind of a Mnemonist: A Little Book About a Vast Memory.* Cambridge, Mass.: Harvard University Press, 1987.

Myers, David G. *Intuition: Its Powers and Perils.* New Haven, Conn: Yale University Press., 2004.

Neisser, Ulric, Gwyneth Boodoo, Thomas J. Bouchard Jr., A. Wade Boykin, Nathan Brody, Stephen J. Ceci, Diane F. Halpern, et al. "Intelligence: Knowns and Unknowns." *American Psychologist* 51, no. 2 (Feb 1996): 77-101.

Pashler, Harold, Mark McDaniel, Doug Rohrer, and Robert Bjork. "Learning Styles: Concepts and Evidence." *Psychological Science in the Public Interest* 9, no. 2 (Dec 2008): 105–119.

Pinker, Steven. *The Language Instinct: How the Mind Creates Language.* New York: Perennial Press, 2000.

Rosenbaum, R. Shayna, Stefan Köhler, Daniel L. Schacter, Morris Moscovitch, Robyn Westmacott, Sandra E. Black, Fuqiang Gao, and Endel Tulving. "The Case of K.C.: Contributions of a Memory-impaired Person to Memory Theory." *Neuropsychologia* 43 (2005): 989–1021.

Sacks, O. *The Man Who Mistook His Wife for a Hat and Other Clinical Tales.* New York: Touchstone Books, 1998.

Skinner, Burrhus Frederic. *Beyond Freedom and Dignity.* New York: Knopf/Random House, 1971.

Stanovich, Keith E. *How to Think Straight About Psychology.* 7th ed. Boston, Mass.: Allyn & Bacon, 2004.

Tavris, Carol. *Psychobabble and Biobunk: Using Psychological Science to Think Critically About Popular Psychology.* 3rd ed. Boston, Mass.: Prentice Hall, 2011.

INDEX

Note: Page numbers followed by *g* indicate glossary entries.

A

academic intelligence, v. practical intelligence 67
accents 49, 50
active memory 7. *See also* short-term memory
ADHD (attention-deficit hyperactivity disorder)
    104
air crib 93
Albert (fear conditioning) 83–86, 88
alcohol use and memory 102
Alda, Alan 86
Alex the Parrot 46–49, 111*g*
algorithm 23–25, 111*g*
American Psychologist 88
American Sign Language, animal use of 45
amnesia, anterograde 100–101, 105, 106–107
amygdala 111*g*
    ghrelin receptors in 106
    and memory/learning 100, 103
    and personality 110
analogies, as well-structured problems 33
analytical intelligence 66–67, 111*g*
animal studies
    brain/brain damage 98, 101–102, 104
    language (communication) 44–49
    memory/learning 101–102, 104
    radial arm maze in 101–102, 104
anosognosia 107–108, 111*g*
antecedents of behavior 87
anterior cingulate cortex 110

anterograde amnesia 100–101, 105, 106–107
applied behavior analysis 82, 94, 111*g*
applied behaviorism 93–95
arbitrariness 55, 111*g*
Army Beta test 77–78
attention
    central executive and 10
    divided 6–7, 113*g*
    focused 4–6, 113*g*
    and magic tricks 5–6
    and memory 3–7
attention-deficit hyperactivity disorder (ADHD)
    104
autism spectrum disorder, applied behavior
    analysis of 94
autobiographical memory 11
availability heuristic 29–30, 111*g*
awareness
    of one's body 107–108
    of other people 108

B

Baddeley, Alan 7–10
Bandura, Albert 92
basal ganglia, and procedural memory 102–104
base rates 27, 111*g*
behaviorism 81–95, 112*g*
    applied 82, 93–95
    classical conditioning in 82–87